*For
Tony,
in gratitude*

# IN SEARCH OF
# SWALLOWS & AMAZONS
## Arthur Ransome's Lakeland

**Roger Wardale**

**Copyright** © Roger Wardale, 1996

**Reprinted,** 1997

All Rights Reserved. No part of this publication may be reproduced, stored in a retrieval system, or transmitted in any form or by any means – electronic, mechanical, photocopying, recording, or otherwise – without prior written permission from the publisher.

**Published by** Sigma Leisure – an imprint of
Sigma Press, 1 South Oak Lane, Wilmslow, Cheshire SK9 6AR, England.

**British Library Cataloguing in Publication Data**
A CIP record for this book is available from the British Library.

**ISBN:** 1-85058-481-8


**Typesetting and Design by:** Sigma Press, Wilmslow, Cheshire.


**Cover:** *Main photograph:* Peel Island and Coniston Old Man *(Wild Cat Island and Kanchenjunga);* *inset, upper:* Coniston Old Man from the hidden harbour at Peel Island *(Kanchenjunga from Wild Cat Island)*; *inset, lower:* Coniston Old Man from Beacon Tarn *(Kanchenjunga from Trout Tarn).*
All photographs by Roger Wardale.


**Printed by:** MFP Design & Print

# Acknowledgements

The greatest pleasure I have had in the preparation of this book has come from the help and encouragement which I have received from so many people.

My special thanks must go to John Bell who, on behalf of the Ransome Estate, has allowed me to select so freely amongst Ransome's unpublished diaries, notebooks, sketch-books and letters, as well as permitting me to reproduce extracts from the stories.

Tony Colwell of Jonathan Cape, Ransome's publisher, encouraged me to write *Arthur Ransome's Lakeland* ten years ago, and has been unstinting with his help and support ever since.

The major collection of Ransome papers is held at the Brotherton Library at the University of Leeds and I am grateful for the co-operation of Christopher Sheppard and his staff, particularly Ann Farr whose knowledge and help over the years has proved invaluable. The other notable collection is at Abbot Hall Art Gallery and Museum in Kendal, and I am indebted to Mary Burkett and Gillian Riding for their help, and for allowing me to photograph the Ransome Room. I am also pleased to acknowledge that permission has been given to reproduce material from both collections.

My thanks also go to Vicky Slowe of the Ruskin Museum, Coniston for allowing me to reproduce the photograph I took of the sculpture by Barbara Collingwood. David McNiell, Map Room Assistant at the Royal Geographical Society, was very helpful in supplying me with large scale maps. It was always a pleasure to visit Kendal and Windermere Libraries where the reference librarians were invariably busy, but always helpful.

The surviving members of the Altounyan family told me about Ransome's gift of *Swallows and Amazons.* and of their days at Coniston and Aleppo. I am grateful to Taqui Altounyan, Susie Villard, Mavis Guzelian, the late Roger Altounyan and Brigit Sanders for sharing their memories so freely.

My thanks are due to Ted Alexander, Robin Anderson, Gillian Beevor, Josephine Russell, Sir Oliver Scott and Hazel Vale for allowing me to reproduce their photographs. Ted also managed to fit in a little research on my behalf during his considerable research into Ransome's many homes.

Everyone writing about Ransome during the last ten years owes a debt to Hugh Brogan and Christina Hardyment, who each published a major work to coincide with Ransome's centenary in 1984.

Finally, I would like to express my appreciation to Jim Andrews, Sheila and Rebecca Barton, Elizabeth Berry, John Berry, Helen and Sheila Caldwell, John Cowen, Janet Gnosspelius, Desmond and Dick Kelsall, Adrian Murray, Charlotte Ryton, Dave Sewart, Lin and Suzannah Strange, and Alan Wilkins.

*Roger Wardale*

## Notes on the Photographs

Almost all the photographs were taken during the last thirty years using a Leica camera and 35mm and 90mm lenses. The exception is the print of a possible North Pole which came from a single frame of a cine film. My aim has always been, as far as possible, to photograph a scene as Ransome knew it and as he described it in his books. Most have been chosen to fit a particular extract from the text and another section shows his various homes as they are today.

Unless otherwise credited, all photographs are by the author.

# Contents

**Rio Bay – at the centre of Arthur Ransome's Lakeland**

# Introduction

The small girl balanced precariously on top of a rock beside an island on Coniston Water, and called out, 'Look at me, Mummy. I'm on Titty's rock!'

A few feet above her on an outcrop of rock that overlooked the island's little harbour, a stranger picnicking with her own children smiled to herself and said nothing. The amused onlooker knew just what the child meant, for she was Titty Guzelian whom Arthur Ransome had 'borrowed' for the classic adventure he wrote originally for her family. The girl on the rock was slipping between make-believe and reality, as readers have been doing ever since Ransome began to conjure magic in *Swallows and Amazons*. Such is the power of the imagery in Ransome's books that for more than sixty years people have gone searching for the 'secret' places which have so attracted them, convinced that they are to be found somewhere. In my own explorations, I have climbed the waterfall as Titty and Roger did in *Swallowdale*, peered in at the glassless window of 'The Dogs' Home' like Dorothea in *The Picts and the Martyrs*, and splashed across the Wade to the real island in *Secret Water*, but nothing compares with the thrill of landing in Wild Cat Island's hidden harbour.

My introduction to Arthur Ransome came through Derek (Uncle Mac) McCulloch's brilliant readings on BBC Children's Hour before I was old enough to read the stories myself. Once I had tackled *The Big Six* on my own, I began to devour the others as soon as they appeared on the shelves of the local library. I kept renewing each book until a fresh one arrived, so that I was never without one or other of the series at home. In those gloomy days of post-war austerity, Ransome's stories were at the height of their popularity. Of course I read books by other writers, but there was something so special about Ransome's stories, some extra quality, that they made me feel sure the lake must really exist. I was puzzled, however, by the maps in Badderley's *Lake District* for none of the real lakes looked the right shape.

Finally, after much pleading on my part, my mother raised the money by doing a little B&B and took me to Bowness-on-Windermere, which we chose because it looked as if it might be Rio. I remember *The Lakes Express* from Euston crawling at a walking pace all the way from Oxenholm to Windermere in a steady drizzle, before finally arriving two hours late. A fine rain was still falling the following morning when we walked down to Bowness Bay and into the make-believe world of the Swallows and Amazons. A steamer was about to leave the pier, rowing boats were milling about in the rain, and we could see past the boat sheds to Long Island. We sat in a shelter overlooking the bay

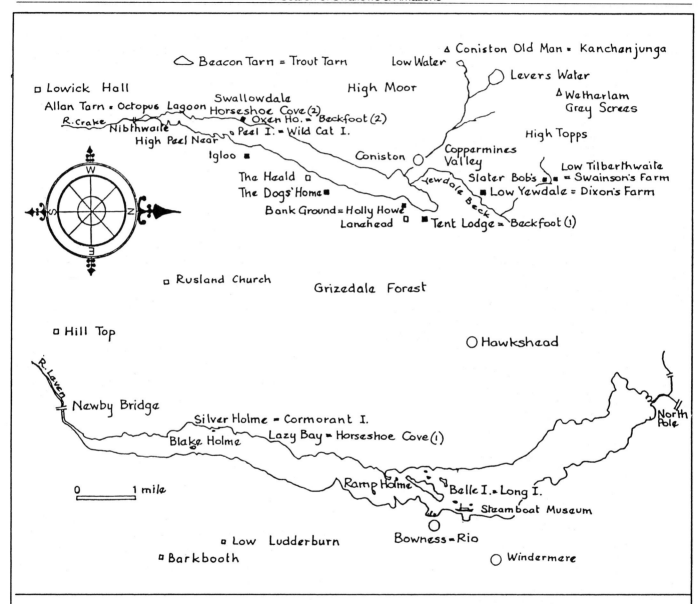

Windermere and Coniston Water : Arthur Ransome's Lakeland

for hours and the rain did not matter one bit! When at last it stopped, we went on a fruitless search for Holly Howe. We had more success to the north of Bowness when we followed Rayrigg Road to the bay now occupied by Windermere Steamboat Museum. There, floating in the bay, was the houseboat. I took a photograph, and just in case it did not 'come out', we both sat on the wall and drew it.

I wrote to Mr Ransome and asked if the boat I had seen really was the houseboat and if he was Captain Flint. 'Please would you tell me where all the other places are,' I added, 'so that on my next holiday I could visit them.' After a while, he responded with the celebrated reply he sent to all such inquirers:

> The only way to keep a secret (your own and other people's) is NEVER to answer a question. But you seem good at guessing. All the places in the books are to be found, but not arranged quite as in the ordnance maps. You seem to be just the reader for those books. I am glad you like them.
>
> With best wishes from
> Arthur Ransome

'All the places in the books are to be found . . .' I felt as if Arthur Ransome had issued a personal challenge and I made up my mind to be equal to it – although it was to be another six years before I had the opportunity to return to the Lake District. The photograph of the houseboat came out very well and this started my collection. I photographed the boatsheds in Rio Bay and then I had the good fortune to discover the secret of Peel Island from Collingwood's *The Lake Counties*. In the books, the question of essential supplies was answered by the presence of some nearby farm, but identifying the various farms, was a difficult problem. In 1966 I wrote again, telling Mr Ransome of my collection of photographs and asking for more help. To my surprise, Evgenia replied:

> My husband has been a very sick man for the last six or seven years. Lately his health has deteriorated still further. He is in Hospital at present and quite unable to deal with his correspondence.

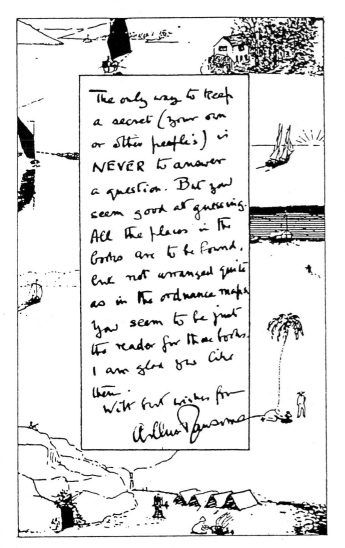

**Ransome's illustrated card**

The Lake District is the background of the *Swallows and Amazons* stories but it is rather more like it used to be in the days of Dr Ransome's own early childhood than it is today. He had deliberately mixed up his topography and rolled up into one lake, Coniston and Windermere so as to include the best features of both; he called Coniston Old Man Kanchenjunga, Bowness-on-Windermere Rio, one of the tiny (I believe nameless) islets in the southern half of Windermere Cormorant Island and made Wild Cat Island partly from Blake Holme on Windermere and partly from Peel Island on Coniston; except for these few you will not be able to find 'exact' spots though you will find coves, bays and promontories closely enough resembling those described in the books if you drift along the shores in a boat and scenery like that of High Tops *(sic)* or High Moor if you walk on Furness fells.

The houses and farms were put onto *Swallows and Amazons* map just as and where the stories demanded them and the names like Atkinson's, Dixon's or Tyson's given to them because these are the typical and most common for the district. And while almost any old traditional farm would do for the purpose of your photography – the difficulty is to find them.

Since the end of the war the District has been in a fever of pulling down, converting, modernising and generally disfiguring old buildings and replacing the farms with factory-like structures and replacing decent houses and cottages with suburban villas and bungalows all glaring with acres of so-called picture windows and bristling with forests of T.V. aerials.

With the roads being continually straightened and widened, with unsightly camping and caravan sites being developed on all sides, with the ever increasing numbers of motor boats on the lakes and the hoards of the wrong kind of tourist visiting the District nowadays it will be soon difficult to imagine that it has ever been as quiet and peaceful as Dr Ransome described it in his books.

Yours sincerely
Evgenia Ransome
Mrs Arthur Ransome

All this was rather misleading, but whether intentionally so I am not sure. There are several locations fitting their description, although others seem to have been combined, like the fictional lake itself. At least two of the farms have characteristics which enable them to be identified with particular buildings. Since that first holiday I have returned to the Lake District time and time again and spent hours 'Ransome-hunting' or revisiting favourite haunts in search of better photographs, the best of which appear in this book

In 1969 Taqui Altounyan's childhood memoir *In Aleppo Once* included a chapter which gave away some secrets of the origin of the stories and the real children involved. Ransome's centenary in 1984 brought the first of the related literature, Hugh Brogan's biography and Christina Hardyment's *Arthur Ransome and Captain Flint's Trunk*. My own book, *Arthur Ransome's Lakeland* appeared in 1986 and its companion, *Arthur Ransome's East Anglia*, two years later. The incomplete 13th Swallows and Amazons book, *Coots in the North*, together with some short stories and a couple of chapters from his unfinished Victorian novel, was also published in 1988. I published a book about Ransome's sailing life, named after his favourite yacht, *Nancy Blackett*, in 1991, and Claire Kendall-Price's book of walks, *In the Footsteps of the Swallows and Amazons*, came out in 1993.

In preparing this book I have returned to primary sources in presenting an account of the origins of the Lake Country books, their characters and their setting. Memories are at best selective and subjective, and I have looked for contemporary written evidence wherever possible. The Brotherton Collection at the University of Leeds holds the diaries of both Ransome and his wife as well as his pocket books. In addition there are 300 letters which he wrote to his mother and drafts for letters to all manner of people, as well as correspondence from his friends accumulated over

**Low Yewdale Farm, 1908.** This early photograph by Arthur Ransome dates from the summer he spent at the farm and shows Dora Collingwood, Mrs Bennett, the farmer's wife and a servant. The photograph was probably taken to mark the end of Ransome's visit, on the day following Dora Collingwood's refusal of marriage. *By kind permission of the executors of the Tabitha Lewis estate.*

the years. Ransome wrote several accounts of the origin of *Swallows and Amazons* and drafts of these survive. In addition there are hundreds of little photographs and negatives. The Abbot Hall Gallery in Kendal has his sketch-books, hand-made Christmas cards from friends and admirers and yet more photographs, as well as the journal of his lifelong friend, Dora Collingwood.

Unfortunately there are gaps in the sequence of letters to his mother, and none of the diaries for the crucial months before he started to write *Swallows and Amazons* contain much of value. Ransome's later accounts of the origins of them differ according to when they were prepared. *How Swallows and Amazons Came to be Written* seems to have been composed quite soon after publication in England in order to introduce the book to American readers. Ransome returned to the subject again shortly afterwards with *Letter to a Friend*, which he did not publish, and finally, when working on his *Autobiography* thirty years later, he wrote an account which was edited out of the text when it was finally published in 1976 and has not appeared anywhere in print.

We may never be sure how long Ransome had been planning *Swallows and Amazons* before he began the actual writing, or of the extent to which he drew upon his young friends and acquaintances when fashioning his characters. Ransome claimed that by writing children's books he was able to have the best of childhood over again. He might have added that by writing about the Lake District he was able to revisit the best of the Lake Country as well.

**Titty's Rock.** *She took her shoes off and paddled across to the big rock on one side of the harbour. She climbed to the top of it, and lay there, looking down to the foot of the lake and watching the steamer swing in towards the distant pier. And just then she saw the dipper.* **Swallows and Amazons** (Peel Island 1995. The author's dinghy is in the harbour)

# Chapter One

# Arthur Ransome and the Lake District

Although both his father and his grandfather came from the Lake District, Arthur Ransome was born and grew up in Leeds where his father was Professor of History at the Yorkshire College (now the University of Leeds). Not everyone can be born in the Lake District and so to make amends, in the spring of 1884 Cyril Ransome carried his young son to the summit of Coniston Old Man when he was still only a few weeks old. The professor was essentially a countryman. He was a keen field naturalist, and a good shot, but above all he loved fishing and had a passion for the Lake Country.

From about the age of seven until Cyril Ransome's death in 1897, young Arthur spent the long summer vacations with his family at Swainson's Farm in the hamlet of High Nibthwaite near the foot of Coniston Water. Swainson's Farm lies at the very foot of the fells, only a couple of minutes from the shore of the lake. The fells themselves are gentle and covered in bracken. The whole family thought of it as a 'magical place'. For almost three months of the year they became lake country folk. The professor fished and his wife painted her water-colours, which left the four children to be 'free in paradise'. Sometimes they rowed a mile up the lake to Peel Island and picnicked, while their father drifted along the shore in the boat

and forgot to eat his sandwiches. In his autobiography Ransome recalls making friends with the animals, the postman, gamekeepers, charcoal-burners, fishermen and the odd poacher or two. Those timeless days spent on the lake or in the pebbly shallows by the boat landing became the stuff of dreams, and the dream was to remain with Arthur throughout his life. The children helped with hay making, turned the butter churn and tickled trout under the tiny bridge. When at last it was time to go, Arthur returned to Leeds carrying a large cardboard box with partitions that contained caterpillars, newts and lizards, or jars of minnows destined for the aquarium.

Lake District summers have more than their share of wet days, and on such days it was their mother's habit to read aloud to the children, while the professor, unable to fish, spent his time writing history books. In his *Autobiography* Ransome says that his mother enjoyed reading aloud and read extremely well. He mentions Kipling's *Jungle Book*, *Lorna Doone*, *The Hunting of the Snark*, *Alice* and books by Charles Kingsley and Andrew Lang. Their own special book was the Norse saga *Thorstein of the Mere* by W.G. Collingwood because it was set in the nearby valley of the River Crake and 'their' island. In 1896 a chance encounter on Peel Island enabled the Ransome family and the Collingwoods to meet for the first time and picnic together.

Back home in Leeds, Arthur had a succession of tutors. He was a lively, sensitive and mischievous little boy, who with his friend Ric Eddison contrived to make life almost unbearable for the unfortunate young men employed to teach them. When he was nine he was sent to prep school at The Old College in Windermere. His undiscovered short-sight meant that he was considered a duffer at games, and because the school was one where boxing and cricket were strongly encouraged, Arthur became the butt of both boys and teachers. The miseries of school could only be forgotten briefly when he went for Sunday lunch to his Great Aunt Susan, who lived at The Terrace above Windermere railway station. What small pleasures were to be had at school came from his love of the countryside. On formal school walks he used to linger behind for as long as he dared in order to listen to the music of a beck as it tumbled through the woods towards the lake. One of his letters home told of his success as a conjuror and asked for some rats or mice in a cage as 'a lot of the boys are getting pets'. Once he made a token attempt to ran away, but he did not get far before being brought back exhausted by the Ullswater coach.

Arthur's abiding memory of his days at The Old College was of the great frost of 1895, when Windermere froze for a month, and the boys were allowed to spend day after day on the ice. They would pile their food on a toboggan and run down the hill into Bowness. Arthur had learnt to skate at Leeds and suddenly found himself in the unfamiliar position of being better at something than the other boys, many of whom had never skated before. He remembered an ox being roasted in Bowness Bay and a coach and horses crisscrossing the ice-bound lake. On Sundays, train loads of day-trippers from Manchester and Liverpool poured out of the station and down the hill until it was estimated that there were more then 20,000 people on the ice. Ice-yachts skimmed over the ice, keeping well away from the crowds gathered near the bands that accompanied the figure-skaters. The boys stayed on until it was dark, when the bay was alight with lanterns and torches.

The Nibthwaite holidays continued until his father's early death from complications that had developed after a fall caused by fishing in the dark. Arthur managed to scrape into his father's public school and had the good fortune at Rugby to come under the influence of a master who discovered the boy's hope for a literary career and actively encouraged him. This encouragement was not welcomed by his mother who thought her eldest son should settle for a steady job. Arthur had been reading since the age of four, and his first book, about a desert island, was completed when he was still only eight. By the time he was seventeen he had a very good idea of what he wanted to do with his life, but first he had to get through university. He had pursued science for less than two terms at Yorkshire College, when he came across the *Life of William Morris*. At once he was captivated by Morris and his friends who had devoted their lives to making things of great beauty. He made up his mind to put aside what could only be a second-best career in science and pursue his ambition to become a writer. After persuading his mother to allow him to go to London, he took a job as office boy for a publishing firm.

At first there was little opportunity for writing, but when he joined the Unicorn Press so as to have more free time, he began in earnest to put pen to paper. Most of his early outpourings ended up on the fire, and on one occasion he had so much to burn that he set his mother's chimney alight. He was encouraged by some early sales to magazines and in 1903, as soon as he had been with the Unicorn Press long enough to be given a holiday, he headed north on the overnight train for Coniston.

Ransome booked himself into Bank House in the village and paid £1 for his week's lodging. A chance meeting with W.G. Collingwood, who found him lying on a rock in the middle of the Coppermines Beck, had a profound effect upon his life. 'Are you alive, young man?' asked Collingwood, for the body on the rock appeared dead. On learning that Ransome had been trying to write poetry, he invited him to call at his home at Lanehead on the other side of Coniston Water. It took all week for Ransome to summon enough courage to take up the invitation, but on his last evening he presented himself at Lanehead only to find the family entertaining friends to dinner. In spite of his untimely arrival he was warmly welcomed and told that next time he should call as soon as he arrived at Coniston.

Back in London, Ransome left the Unicorn Press and took lodgings in Chelsea. He was still only nineteen, and by selling articles to magazines, he managed to make enough money – or nearly enough – to live. The following year he was invited to stay with the Collingwoods who seemed to him the living embodiment of William Morris's ideal. W.G. Collingwood was a writer, painter, antiquary and archeologist. Ransome called him 'The Skald' in recognition of his Norse scholarship and said, 'There never was a man who did so much for other people'. His wife was a painter of portrait miniatures. Of all his friendships, that of the Collingwood family was the most important to Ransome. Above all else, they gave him the encouragement that he did not find in his own family.

The three eldest children – Dora, Barbara and Robin – all planned to follow a career in the Arts. Frequently Ransome and the girls went off in a boat with a picnic tea. At other times they worked indoors. A glimpse of the 20-year old Ransome is to be found in Dora Collingwood's journal where she noted that in the evening he took Barbara and herself out into the garden and tried to make them see fairies. Naturally he fell in love with the girls, but especially with Barbara. Perhaps it was his high-spirited enthusiasm, coupled with a lack of worldliness, which made the girls call him 'Toad'. It was to be more than a month before he could drag himself away. Even then Mrs Collingwood had to pack his case because his things were in 'hopeless confusion'. His going left a 'large gap in the household'.

During the next few years he was to see a great deal of the Collingwoods. In 1905 the whole Ransome family spent three weeks at How Head, almost next door. He developed the habit of dropping in on whatever the Collingwoods were doing and staying for hours on end. For their part, the girls found Ransome interesting and unusual. 'He really is a dear in spite of his eccentricities. He is so nice and utterly different from any man I know . . .' confided Dora, but she recognised that he was self-centred and she also commented on his thoughtlessness. He proposed to both girls more than once, and Barbara took a long time to make up her mind before refusing him. They remained friends for the rest of their lives.

No one can be sure when Ransome learnt to sail. At Nibthwaite the Ransomes only had the use of a rowing boat, and so his first lessons were probably aboard the *Swallow* which Dora, Barbara and Robin Collingwood sailed and which they kept in the boathouse below Lanehead.

For the next four years Ransome's life followed a

pattern. The winters were spent in London, hard at work, but each summer he set off for the north. He published some books of essays which are perhaps best forgotten. He read widely, and already – so far as his modest income would allow – he had become a book collector. Life in Bohemian London agreed with him. He made a number of friends from among the literati of the time, including the poet Edward Thomas, who shared the same lodgings for a while. Three summers he spent at Wall Nook Farm near Cartmel in order to be near his friend the poet and playwright, Gordon Bottomley. He was given a bedroom overlooking the fells and fed very well for his £1 per week. At this time he developed an amazing appetite for his landlady's home-made marmalade, and years later, marmalade was to make regular appearances in his books.

While he was at Wall Nook he wrote four simple children's books: *Pond and Stream*, *The Child's Book of the Seasons*, *Things in our Garden*, and *Highways and Byways in Fairyland*. Ransome tried to devote his weekdays to writing and at weekends he walked fifteen miles to see Barbara Collingwood at Lanehead, calling on his way for a pint at the Hark to Melody in Haverthwaite and another at the Red Lion at Lowick Bridge. Often his companion on these walks was the poet Lascelles Abercrombie, who also stayed at Wall Nook. After a day spent on the lake they would walk back in the dark.

In 1908 he stayed at a farm in Low Yewdale, beside the Yewdale Beck. By now he had acquired a tent which in fine weather he would pitch on a mound beside the beck a few yards upstream. In his autobiography he refers to 'a countryside I can call my own' and speaks of otters playing in the moonlight, the heron beside the lake shore and corncrakes in the fields below the bobbin mill. He seems to have been more at home in the valleys than on the high fells. He renewed his boyhood friendship with the charcoal burners in the coppice woodlands and made new friends from among the Gypsies. Ransome also joined the young men practising Cumberland and Westmorland wrestling for the Grasmere Sports. All this while he continued to haunt the Collingwoods, who for their part always made him welcome.

After Barbara's refusal of marriage, Ransome seems to have made a habit of proposing to a variety of girls, just for practice. Unfortunately, when he proposed to Ivy Walker in the hot-house atmosphere of artistic London, she ignored her family's advice, broke off her engagement to her cousin, and accepted him. After their marriage in 1909 the couple travelled north to meet Ransome's Lake Country friends. The visit was a failure and three days later they were back in Petersfield, Hampshire, where he and Ivy had set up home. The following May their daughter Tabitha was born. Later that summer Ransome had a holiday camping in the Lanehead garden and on Peel Island. Ivy, Tabitha and their Jamaican nurse joined them in October and they occupied Lanehead for a couple of months during the time that the Collingwoods were away. For a fortnight in 1912 Dora Collingwood stayed with them in their home in Wiltshire and found it 'a quaint and unusual household'. She liked Ivy and enjoyed her stay with them, but she was glad to get away from people who 'live on their emotions to such an extent'.

This was the period of his life when Ransome devoted himself to literary criticism and produced *A History of Story Telling* and *Edgar Allen Poe*. It was his book *Oscar Wilde* which landed the horrified author in a celebrated court case. His alleged libel was successfully defended and Ivy revelled in the public attention, but the experience left Ransome determined never to write anything which could possibly bring him up against the law again. Instead he became interested in folk tales.

In 1913 Ransome left for Russia to collect Russian fairy stories. He loved his little daughter, but he recognised that he would never be happy living with Ivy. He decided that a clean break would be for the best, and knew Ivy would not be able to follow him to Russia. He appears to have had no difficulty teaching himself the language from children's reading books, and in a couple of years he had collected enough stories to retell to English children in *Old Peter's Russian Tales*, which was published in 1916.

By now Ransome had become a journalist, due more to a sense of patriotism than anything. During the Great War he remained in Russia to send eye-witness reports of the Revolution to the *Daily News* and later to the *Manchester Guardian*. Recently it has been suggested that Ransome might have been a spy for the Russian secret police, and contemporary accounts indicate that his information on British foreign policy was 'very important' to Lenin. Certainly Ransome was well known at the Kremlin, where he played chess with Lenin. At one time he was actually suspected of being a British agent, but he was probably no more than a mediator who believed that Russia should be left to sort out her own problems without intervention from the west. It was while he was gathering bulletins from the Bolsheviks that he met and fell in love with Trotsky's secretary. She was the 'tall, jolly girl', Evgenia Petrovna Shelepina, who was to become his second wife. Evgenia was a high-born young woman whose family lived in a large house next door to the Minister of Foreign Affairs. She had received a privileged education, and during the time Ransome was writing the stories, she was his harshest critic and his most loyal supporter. One who knew them both at this time was Bruce Lockhart, the Acting Consul-General at Moscow, who described Ransome as 'a Don Quixote with a walrus moustache' and Evgenia as 'extremely able and tactful'. No one interested in this eventful period of Ransome's life should miss Hugh Brogan's *The Life of Arthur Ransome* which covers it in detail.

**Arthur Ransome by Jan Neiman**

Lockhart enabled Evgenia to leave Russia by giving her a British passport and for several years Ransome and Evgenia lived in the Baltic states of Estonia and Latvia while he continued to send reports of the political situation to the *Manchester Guardian*. With his sprig of heather from Peel Island and a lucky stone from the summit of Coniston Old Man, Ransome seems to have been marking time until Ivy should agree to a divorce and he could return to the Lake Country and fishing. Meanwhile there were compensations for living in eastern Europe, and after two summers sailing small and unsuitable craft, they had the well-known *Racundra* built for cruising in the Baltic. Their cruise from Riga to Helsingfors and back, with Carl Sehmel as crew, gave Ransome *Racundra's First Cruise,* which is still considered one of the finest accounts of small boat cruising. The name *Racundra* has long puzzled people. It is made up of RA (Ransome) C (Carl Sehmel) UND (and) RA (Evgenia). Ransome was still married to Ivy and for delicacy, throughout the book Evgenia is referred to as The Cook. Sehmel used to recall with amusement that the pipe-smoking cook slept with pet snakes in her bunk. Eventually Ivy agreed to a divorce and Ransome and Evgenia were married at Reval (now Tallin) in Estonia in May 1924. A year later they settled in the Lake District.

For £550 the Ransomes bought Low Ludderburn, a stone cottage three hundred years old with nearly two acres of land overlooking the Winster valley. The cottage is 400 feet above sea level and about six miles along narrow, winding lanes to the south of Windermere town. Ransome wrote joyfully to his mother:

> From the terrace in front of the house you can see Arnside and a strip of sea under the Knott. Away to the left you can see Ingleborough, and from the fell just behind the house you can see Ambleside and all the lake hills. It contains two rooms on the ground floor, plus a scullery hole. Two rooms upstairs. A lean-to in bad repair, capable of being turned into a first-rate kitchen. a huge two-story barn in first-rate condition, stone built, at present with stables below and the top part which has a double door opening on the road is used to put up a Morris Cowley. Water from a Roman well just behind the house, our title deeds giving us the right to lay a pipe from it to the house. a lot of apples, damsons, gooseberries, raspberries, currants, and the whole orchard white with snowdrops and daffodils just coming.
>
> Blemishes. Very low beams in the rooms. A good deal to be done to make it really nice. But it is a stout place . . .

Evgenia was just as enthusiastic. What neither of them mentioned in their letters was that their home was isolated and without electricity or telephone. Life in such a place would have been impossible without a car, and so they acquired what Ransome called 'a perambulating biscuit tin' which 'rattles about beautifully'. The lanes around the cottage require care, and only two days after he had taken over the car, Ransome ran into a wall. Evgenia was the practical one, overseeing the conversion of the upper room of the barn into a wonderfully light and airy workroom with a new wooden floor, a fireplace and a window looking across the valley, at a cost of a further £125. Having seen to this improvement, she began to take the garden in hand.

At that time the *Manchester Guardian* still regarded Ransome as a valuable foreign correspondent, and the paper secured for him a regular income. During the first few years at Ludderburn, he was sent to Egypt, Sudan, Russia and China; visits he made with increasing reluctance as they became settled into their Lakeland home. He was also called upon to contribute, when the occasion demanded, leading

**Low Ludderburn, by Roger Wardale after a watercolour by Edith Ransome**

articles on foreign politics. It must have been very lonely for Evgenia, living in an isolated cottage in a foreign country during Ransome's months abroad. It is not surprising that she made a point of carefully recording in her diary the time at which the postman called each day! Shopping in Windermere involved a hilly round trip of twelve miles and it was just as well that Evgenia quickly became accustomed to walking uphill.

They both delighted in the wildlife which surrounded their home and enjoyed watching the nesting redstarts and spotted flycatchers. Both their diaries have records of sightings of goldcrests, long-tailed tits and red squirrels. Ransome had obtained permission to fish the upper reaches of the River Winster before they had moved in, and he found that he had only to go through the orchard and down the footpath for half a mile or so in order to reach the best stretch. He was soon writing happily to his mother that he had caught eight trout in one afternoon. Fishing was a pastime that Evgenia could share and she often accompanied him on trips on the lake and to the nearby rivers. Among their friends, she gained a reputation for making the most delicious fish soup from perch. They bought a rowing boat when they first moved to Ludderburn, and from 1929 they could sail to the head of Windermere for tea at the Wateredge Hotel in an hour. Favourite picnic spots were Blake Holme and one of the Lilies of the Valley islands behind Belle Isle. They also entered *Swallow* in 'all-comers' races and would return from a sail very wet, but having thoroughly enjoyed the little craft battling with the wind and water.

Half a mile across the valley at Barkbooth he found a fishing companion in Colonel Kelsall. Together they devised a means of signalling across the valley using square and triangular boards hung from hooks in their walls, so that they could be read without leaving their homes. Their code included messages such as 'Have you any worms?' and 'Are you going fishing?'

Charles Renold from Cheadle in Cheshire was another fisherman with whom Ransome formed a close friendship and other regular visitors to Ludderburn were Ted Scott, son of the editor of the *Manchester Guardian*, and his son Dick, who were duly introduced to the pleasures of Lake Windermere. Ransome began a regular fishing column for the *Manchester Guardian*, which gave him an excuse to fish over a wider area. He fished the Cumberland Derwent, the Hodder, the Ribble, the Eden and the Dove. He also commented on country matters and these articles show him to be an environmentalist ahead of his time. More than once he used his column to contribute an attack on speeding motor-boats on Lake Windermere:

Towards the end of April motor boats appear, and now, when the fishing should be really worth while, these monstrous creatures with a crew of one or perhaps two are roaring up and down the lake, creating a vibration that can be felt from one side of the lake to the other and making the surface of the lake a patchwork quilt (there is no other way of describing the effect of the oil they exude).

He also spoke out strongly against the practice of tarring country roads:

Not far from where I am writing there is a delightful little beck flowing out into Morecambe Bay, full of decent little trout and frequented by salmon in the spawning season. A few days ago, thanks to the road authorities, there was so much tar on the roads that the rains blackened the stream, in the words of the local postman who actually saw the dead fish floating down it. If this sort of thing is to go on unchecked it will not be long before our trout and salmon rods will be treasured in museums as 'instruments used in the early twentieth century in the capture of now extinct aquatic creatures.'

These were unusual outbursts: more typical is this example of Ransome's ability to express his love of the lake country:

So far, everywhere on the rivers, the main pleasure of fishing has been that of being at the waterside, where, after all, there is much to be seen besides fish. This is the season when a man may see a cloud of long-tailed tits blowing through the leafless bushes that overhang the river. Wrens are busy and show the fisherman where they are and what they are about by going into shrill hysterics and scolding him as if they were prepared to drive him out of the river. Dippers are building. Herons, of course, are about as usual, but I have not seen a kingfisher this year.

Fifty of the best of these fishing pieces were brought

together in book form and published in 1929 under the title of *Rod and Line*. This delightful collection is thought to be one of the most important of fishing books, and it has been followed more than sixty years later with another collection, *Arthur Ransome on Fishing*, in which Jeremy Swift, himself a fisherman, also contributes a long introduction to Ransome's fishing life.

Frequently Ransome's only diary entries were records of the arrival of the swallows, the first blooming of the daffodils or the catching of eight trout in the River Crake. However he was not above taking his gun to any rabbit or pheasant unwise enough to stray on to his land. At New Year 1928 he and Evgenia, climbed through the snow to the top of Ludderburn Hill so that they could hear the sound of church bells from across the valley. It became an annual celebration, though life at Ludderburn was not entirely idyllic. Evgenia fought a constant battle against

marauding sheep who had developed a fancy for her flowers, and on one occasion a plague of field mice that threatened to overrun the cottage. Their cat Winkle gave birth to three silver-grey kittens which they took down to The Cat Show at Crystal Palace, where the trio were Highly Commended. Two of the kittens, Polly and Podge, they kept.

The workroom was Ransome's special pride. The large worktable was covered by a grey blanket and littered with all manner of keepsakes as well as his writing things and the typewriter. There were big shelves teeming with books, files and rows of diaries, and around the large room were comfortable chairs, while looking down from high on a wall was a stuffed fish. It was in this workroom that he wrote *Swallows and Amazons*, carrying the manuscript up to his bedroom at night so as to be able to lean out and touch it from his bed. Once he had a bad fall while going down the steep hill at Birks Brow, 'listening to

'Exercise' by Evgenia Ransome

'Rest' by Evgenia Ransome

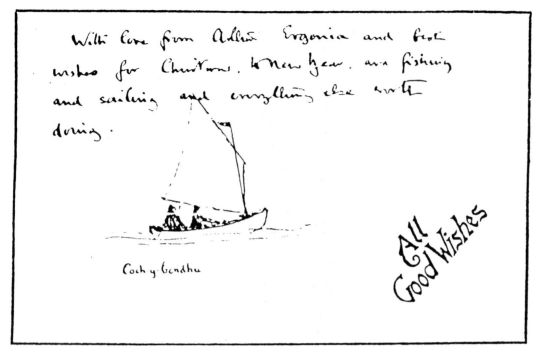

With love from Arthur Evgenia and best wishes for Christmas, the New Year, and fishing and sailing and everything else worth doing.

Coch-y-bondhu

All Good Wishes

**Christmas card**

to put on weight, give up journalism for good and never use aluminium cooking pots again.

There were still plenty of interesting diversions to take his mind off the worry of the moment. In 1933, when Charles and Margaret Renold became interested in sailing, they camped on one of the Windermere islands and were taken sailing in *Swallow*. The following winter their own boat was built by Crossfields of Arnside, who had built *Swallow*, and Ransome enthusiastically supervised the building.

Dorothea', and had to crawl more than half a mile home with a broken ankle. For some time after the accident he was unable to indulge in his habit of pacing up and down the workroom while thinking.

The Ludderburn years were the most creative of Ransome's life, but there was a price to pay. He had developed a duodenal ulcer, brought on by worrying over money. Thereafter he never went anywhere without his small leather attache case containing bottles of bismuth, wholemeal biscuits and some milk, taken at regular intervals. Publisher's deadlines and bouts of depression, which seem to have overtaken him at some stage in the preparation of every book, only served to make matters worse. He sought help in Harley Street and tried a variety of cures without a great deal of success until he was ordered

The little boat was given the name *Coch-y-bonddhu* after a fishing fly, but from the first it was always called *Cocky*. Ransome noted in his diary that when *Cocky* raced *Swallow* she beat her by the length of Belle Isle. Later that summer Ransome raced *Cocky* again: 'Genia was cold and found *Cocky* too small and generally did not enjoy herself. It was a pity we tried it. But the little boat sailed jolly well. One of the big ones was dismasted.' The Renolds preferred fishing to small boat sailing and somehow *Cocky* became Ransome's. His internal problems always seemed to clear up when he went sailing on the Broads and although *Racundra* had been sold in order to buy the cottage, the Ransomes had never given up the hope of being able to continue the sort of cruising which came to an end when they returned to England.

By the summer of 1935 the Swallows books were selling well and Ransome was able to buy a 7-ton cutter and rename it *Nancy Blackett*. Ludderburn and *Swallow* were sold and they rented a house close to the River Orwell in Suffolk. He managed to spend a good deal of time afloat during the next four summers and once made a notable North Sea crossing to Holland in order to be sure of the details of the unsought voyage in *We Didn't Mean to Go to Sea*. With the outbreak of the Second World War he became land-bound again and a letter from Barbara Collingwood, married and settled near Coniston, full of Lake District news made him think longingly of the lakes once more. He said in a letter to his mother in August 1940

> . . . the area is full of holiday-makers asking the way, as all sign posts have been removed, even the little board on the Hawkshead road that said 'To the Tarns'. I must say it all made me very homesick for a look at the lakes and a run or rather crawl up to the top of the Old Man, but I can't possibly stir from here in the present circuses *(sic)*.

The circumstances changed much more quickly than he could have foreseen. Evgenia suffered much more from the air-raids and disturbed nights than her husband, and when they learned that they could be turned out of their home at twenty-four-hours notice, Evgenia agreed to return to the Lake District. A couple of months later Ransome wrote a very different letter to his mother:

> . . . being back in the lakes makes everything look pretty good. You know I had quite made up my mind that nothing would get Genia to come back. I don't think anything would except the war, which of course got lively in our parts very early on . . . now she is back, she seems very pleased . . . though the rooms are so tiny that we can't move without hitting our funny-bones. There is none of that shut-in feeling she didn't like at Lane-head, and the house itself has none of the primitive savagery of Ludderburn. First-rate water supply for one thing.

Their new home was The Heald, situated mid-way along the road that runs down the east side of Coniston Water and surrounded by pine trees. With the bungalow went seventeen acres of lovely woodland and half a mile of lake frontage. Close at hand was a wooden jetty to which they could moor *Coch-y-bond-dhu*, which they took north with them.

The Ransomes were optimistic when they set out with Polly and Podge on their journey, and for a while Evgenia felt better, but the reality proved disappointing. For one thing, The Heald was even more isolated than Ludderburn. The nearest shop was in Coniston village five miles around the head of the lake and the weekly shopping expedition to Ulverston involved a trip of 18 miles. Petrol rationing meant that after they had fuelled the electricity generator they had next to no petrol left. Ransome took to a light motor-bike (the Monster), but Evgenia was not so fortunate. The damp weather did not agree with her and the poor soil frustrated her gardening ambitions. Instead she kept chickens.

It was not long before Ransome suffered two ruptures and his doctor told him that his sailing and fell-walking days were over. He could, however, fish *quietly*. For some time he was unable to row his boat, so he painstakingly learnt to fish for Coniston char under sail, as he explained to his mother:

> Last night we had a most luxurious supper on a brace of char, each close to half a pound (big for Coniston) caught by sailing. The trouble comes when you hook your fish sixty to eighty yards way and have to manage sail, rudder, rod, reel and net at one and the same time with only two hands and false teeth. But the thing can be done and last night's supper was the proof of it.

The Ransomes had a hard time at The Heald and by 1945 they were trying unsuccessfully to take up their old life on the East Coast. They could not find suitable property in the area in which they wanted to live and settled in London instead. Ransome commissioned a new boat which he called a 'marine bath-chair' and to which the designer gave the name *Peter Duck.* 'It will be plain *PD,*' grumbled Ransome. They never took to the boat, although it has proved a highly successful design and thirty-eight were built.

After one frustrating summer with the boat, they bought Lowick Hall, only five miles across the valley from the scene of his childhood holidays. Not only did they take on the hall but also the adjacent farm as well and 130 acres. The whole enterprise was financially and physically too much for them. The roof leaked, some of the floors were rotten and the place needed new drainage. After a couple of months Ransome was 'very disheartened' and a year later Evgenia had had enough: 'Genia says she wants to give up Lowick. Impossible with no staff.' Evgenia had never been able to get on with servants. Ransome, however, quickly managed to slip back into his old ways, fishing, sailing *Cocky* on Windermere, playing cards and chess with friends and taking pot-shots at any stoat invading his lawn. But the Lake District was changing. On one occasion while sailing on Windermere, he landed on Blake Holme only to be disturbed by the sound of a radio blaring from the nearby shore. Even at Lowick Hall his peace could be disturbed: 'Large well-dressed girl in garden with two others. When told she really ought not to be in someone else's garden she shouted out that I was a blackguard and a parasite!!!'

They parted with Lowick Hall in 1950, after two years of pouring money into the place, and took a flat in Putney overlooking the Thames. They managed to continue cruising on the South Coast and across the Channel until 1954 when Ransome finally accepted that his sailing days were over. From 1955 until they

finally relinquished their London flat in 1963, they spent the summers in the Lake District and the winters in town. At first they rented Ealinghearth Cottage at Haverthwaite, and then nearby Hill Top which eventually they bought. Ransome managed to continue fishing until 1960, but a fall in 1958 began a long, sad decline. Ever optimistic, he had a go at driving a Morris Minor car as late as 1961, when he was 77. When that failed, he was effectively a prisoner at Hill Top except when friends were able to take him for a drive. Hill Top was yet another remote cottage and quite unsuitable for anyone's final years. Yet he was still able to find pleasure in natural history and a present of a jar of tadpoles and a grass snake brought him 'great delight'.

In 1962 he allowed the BBC to make a filmed serial of *Swallows and Amazons* and, having done so; immediately regretted it, as he told his old sailing friend Colonel Busk:

> . . . horrid children with loathsome voices and so forth . . . and where will they find the brats to be filmed while sailing? And where will they find S and A, the two boats? They have already plumped for the wrong island (with no harbour). In fact general prospect of horror.

The surviving fragment of film showing Titty in a duffel coat and the children wearing life-jackets, seems to support his view.

As Ransome became more frail, he grew increasingly dependent on Evgenia who struggled on with her sciatica for as long as she could. In October 1965, after her second heart attack and Ransome's second stroke, she transferred him to Cheadle Royal Hospital in Manchester where he died eighteen months later. One of his regular visitors during that time was Dick Kelsall. Ransome was desperately ill but his eyes lit up whenever Kelsall spoke of the time when they had all lived in the Winster Valley.

**Swainson's Farm**

**Lanehead**

**Dora Collingwood 1914 by Barbara Collingwood**

**Evgenia with a large pike, Low Ludderburn** (Photo: Arthur Ransome, courtesy Abbot Hall)

*Above:* **The view from Low Ludderburn.** *Below:* **Low Ludderburn Barn where *Swallows and Amazons* was written** (Photo: Ted Alexander)

**Frozen Windermere 1929 with Evgenia and the *Maid Marion*.** (Photo: Arthur Ransome, courtesy Abbot Hall)

**Arthur Ransome aboard a hired yacht on the Norfolk Broads, 1938.** (Photo: Josephine Russell)

**Arthur Ransome with Gillian Beevor on the shore of Coniston Water, 1956.** (photo: Gillian Beevor)

*Above:* **The Heald** (Photo: Ted Alexander).  *Below:* **Lowick Hall** (Photo: Ted Alexander)

**Hill Top** (Photo: Ted Alexander)

**The Ransomes at Hill Top** (Photo: Arthur Ransome, courtesy Abbot Hall)

**Taqui Altounyan, Brigit Sanders and Roger Altounyan, 1985**

# Chapter Two

# The Coming of the Swallows

Anyone looking for the origin of *Swallows and Amazons* will be confronted by Ransome's note, written in 1958, which has appeared in all subsequent editions:

I have been often asked how I came to write *Swallows and Amazons.* The answer is that it had its beginning long, long ago when, as children my brother, my sisters and I spent most of our holidays on a farm at the south end of Coniston. We played in or on the lake or on the hills about it finding friends in the farmers and shepherds and charcoal-burners whose smoke rose from the coppice woods along the shore. We adored the place. Coming to it we used to run down to the lake, dip our hands in and wish, as if we had just seen the new moon. Going away from it we were half-drowned in tears. While away from it, as children and as grown ups, we dreamt about it. No matter where I was, wandering about the world, I used at night to look for the North Star and in my mind's eye, could see the beloved skyline of great hills beneath it. *Swallows and Amazons* grew out of those memories. I could not help writing it. It almost wrote itself.

One of Ransome's earliest published efforts was a series of whimsical little nature books for children. In the third of these, *Pond and Stream* (1906), the Imp and the Elf, having looked at a beck and met a dipper, are drawn towards 'a little rocky island' on the lake.

The book was written shortly after Ransome had become a member of the Collingwood family circle and there is a clear reference to Collingwood's Norse saga *Thorstein of the Mere.*

We ran the boat carefully aground in a pebbly inlet at one end of the island. We take the baskets ashore, and camp in the shadow of a little group of pines . . . As soon as the tea is over we prowl over the rockiness of the little island, and creep among the hazels and pines and tiny oaks and undergrowth . . . When we have picked our way through to the other end, we climb upon a high rock with a flat top to it, and heather growing in its crevices, and here we lie, torpid after our tea, and pretend we are Viking folk from the north who have forced our way here by land and sea, and are looking for the first time upon a lake that no one knew before us.

*Swallows and Amazons* evidently grew out of *Pond and Stream,* for even in this apprentice work there is an almost poetic response to the Lake District. In crossing between reality and imagination, Ransome makes use of a device which was to become one of the strongest features of *Swallows and Amazons*: '*Swallow* and her crew moved steadily southward over a desolate ocean sailed for the first time by white seamen.'

Ransome's carefully prepared note, however, tells only part of the story. The rest lies behind the withheld dedication, 'To the six for whom it was written in exchange for a pair of slippers' – which was omitted from 1948 onwards. After *Pond and Stream*, twenty-two years were to pass before some children that he knew a little, came to his childhood playground at Coniston and their visit gave him the impetus to write *Swallows and Amazons*. These were the children of Dora Collingwood and the Irish-Armenian surgeon Ernest Altounyan, sometimes seen as a rival to Ransome in the affection of the Collingwood sisters. In fact, Dora did not meet Altounyan until after Ransome's first marriage. For some years they had been living in Syria where Altounyan helped his father to run the well-known hospital at Aleppo. Every few years they returned to Coniston to stay at the home of Dora's parents at Lanehead, arriving at the end of April 1928, complete with the family – Taqui (Barbara), Susie, Titty (Mavis), Roger, Bushie (Brigit) and their Armenian nurse.

Altounyan was a sailing enthusiast and had decided his four eldest children were ready to learn to sail. They stayed at Bank Ground, the farm just below their grandparent's home at Lanehead, as the elderly couple were unable to cope with eight visitors for a long stay. Hardly had they established themselves at Bank Ground than Altounyan went off to Barrow in Furness and bought two sturdy dinghies for £15 apiece. Ransome and Altounyan came to an agreement that, when the Altounyans returned to Syria, one of the little boats would become Ransome's and he would pay his share.

From time to time the Ransomes drove over to Coniston and fished for perch, while the children sailed in circles by the Lanehead boathouse. Altounyan saw to it that the children behaved in a proper seamanlike manner. In those days even harmlessly trailing a hand in the water was frowned upon as the behaviour of a tripper. Both Ransome and Altounyan believed that, so far as possible, people should be allowed to discover how to do things for themselves. Taqui and Titty sailed *Mavis*, a narrow white-painted dinghy with a white standing lug sail and a heavy iron centreplate, which must have been almost impossible for 11-year old Taqui to lift. *Mavis* is 13 feet long and had been built at Piel Island near Barrow. Taqui remembers the thrill of jumping aboard *Mavis* and feeling the boat come alive beneath her feet. The other children thought her 'rather a tub'. They preferred *Swallow*, the more attractive dinghy they named after the old Coniston *Swallow* sailed by their parents. *Swallow* was the same length and was also white, but it had a brown top strake and a brown sail. It was much roomier and had no centre-board for Susie and Roger to struggle with. *Swallow* had been built by Crossfields of Arnside shortly before World War One. Susie remembers what an easy boat *Swallow* was to handle and how Uncle Arthur showed them how to fish in the shallow water by the lake shore. Titty loved those windless days spent fishing over the edge of the transom with her legs dangling above the water. Roger used to have the job of keeping *Mavis* bailed out and he preferred splashing around in the tiny dinghy they called *Toob* or *Tub*.

The Altounyans remained at Bank Ground Farm until the following January and generously agreed that they would keep *Mavis* so that Ransome could sail *Swallow*. Shortly before they were due to leave, it was Ransome's birthday, and the following afternoon there were cries of 'Many happy returns,' as Taqui and Titty appeared at Low Ludderburn holding a splendid pair of red leather slippers which they had bought in an Aleppo souk as a present. Their father hid behind the garden wall awaiting developments, for Ransome had said that he was busy and that if Altounyan came at all, he should leave the children behind. Ransome stormed down from his workroom in the barn, but his heavy frown soon melted away and Altounyan felt it safe to come out of hiding. Ransome was touched by the children's gift and by their generosity in allowing him to have *Swallow*. There was a sad parting at Windermere station a couple of days later.

Shortly afterwards Ted Scott of the *Guardian* offered Ransome a large increase in salary if he would go to Berlin for eighteen months as their correspondent. On completion of this tour of duty he would be allowed to return to Manchester and become Literary Editor. Ransome realised that his life was at the crossroads. Never having wanted to become a journalist and aware of the demands that such a career would make, he knew that if he accepted the offer he would probably not be able to write another book. With Evgenia's full support he turned his back on security and resigned. From then on, he decided he would work for the paper only on a freelance basis. Having travelled to Manchester to break the news to his friend, the Ransomes took *Swallow* from the Borwick's boatshed in Bowness Bay for the first time, and went for a sail. On one occasion Ransome wrote that it was during that sail that he had the idea of writing a book in which the heroine would be the little boat itself. He thought what fun they would all have if he could write a book for the Altounyans. He could even use some of their names.

Even though it was early in the year, whenever they had to go to Windermere for shopping or to post articles they managed to have a sail in *Swallow*. On 24th March, three days after that first sail, the diary entry reads 'Began S & A.' The surviving notes show that John, Nancy and Peggy were not his first choice,

but that he had already decided upon the names Susan, Titty and Roger. A couple of pages of notes hidden away in the notebook he later used as the log for his yacht *Nancy Blackett*, which he sailed off the East Coast, reveal some of his first thoughts:

| Swallows | ~~Dick~~ John 12 | Amazons | Jane 13 |
| | Susan 10 | | Mary (proper name Ruth) 12 |
| | Titty 8 | | Tom 3 |
| | Roger 6 | | |

Vic Does not count 1½
Parents to Amazons ~~Smith~~ Walker
Mother of the Swallows  Smith
The Houseboat Man  Turner

The rejected name of Dick is an interesting choice and suggests Dick Scott, the son of his closest friend. The boy visited Ludderburn occasionally and had been staying there a day or so before the Altounyans arrived with their birthday gift. He was introduced to fishing and sailing by Ransome and was about twelve at the time. On another page is a list of chapters:

1. Introductory. Tents & Swallow

2. Preparation. ———————— & collecting outfit

3. Island. First landing

4. Cormorants. Fishing. The Houseboat man. Mother after a sleep.

5. An enemy. The Amazons. The Amazon.. Jane, Ruth (crossed out) Mary

   (Ruthless)

6. Tame without the Amazons. Dick going home. Take the Post. Agreement with mother.

7. The lighthouse and lights.

8. The expedition.

9. Titty alone. The wrong boat.

10. The Amazons on the island. Titty in the boat.

11. _____ _____ Peace with the Amazons.

12. Dick learns of burgled houseboat. Did he do it?

13. Search party conquered by the children who rescue them hospitably.

14. Policeman (crossed out)

15. Titty & the treasure from the houseboat.

16. The second arrow. 'We are prisoners.'

17. The rescue.

18. The Amazons' captive. entertainment by the children. The letter with thanks

19. The discovery of thieves by the children. The number of the car. All help to ―――――-

20. The end.

This is followed by a list of books: *Baltic Pilot*, a German Dictionary, *Brown's Signalling Manual*, *The Mate's Handybook* and *Simple Cooking for Small Households*. A note found with the draft which was dated 1929 indicates a probable development:

| Swallows | | Amazons | |
|----------|----------------------|---------|----------|
| | John 12 | | ~~Jane~~ |
| | Susan 10 | | Nancy 13 |
| | Titty 9 | | ~~Mary~~ |
| | Roger 7 | | Peggy 12 |
| | Victoria (Bridget) 1½ | | Tom 3 |

On 5th April he travelled to London and took half a page of notes and a list of chapter headings to Jonathan Cape who agreed to publish the book when it was finished, though what he really wanted was Ransome's promised collection of essays. Cape agreed to pay an advance of £100. The following day

Ransome celebrated by fishing with friends in Hampshire. Then he returned to Ludderburn and, swept along in a rush of enthusiasm, continued to work on the first draft of *Swallows and Amazons*, begrudging time spent on anything else. He had planned for 200 pages of typescript. By the time he had finished it had reached page 253. One detail Ransome omitted to tell readers in the published version was that Nancy and Peggy had curly hair showing round their red woollen knitted caps. A page of his sketchbook shows a variety of such caps, possibly the work of Evgenia. Ransome noted in his diary his daily output. On 13th April he wrote four pages of 'The First Arrow', and followed this with three pages of 'The Parley', reaching a total of 64 pages completed. On 18th May, just eight weeks after he had started, the job was done. He described the writing in his draft entitled, *How Swallows and Amazons Came to be Written* which was published in the United States to coincide with the American edition:

I was enjoying the writing of this book more than I have ever enjoyed writing any other book in my life. And I think I can put my figure on the thing in it which gave me so much pleasure, it was just this, the way in which the children in it have no firm dividing line between make-believe and reality, but slip in and out of one and the other again and again.

He started the second draft on 7th June, but he also had to begin a series of Saturday articles for the *Manchester Guardian* entitled *Drawn at a Venture* and wrote 2000 words on such varied subjects as The *Birth of a Myth*, *On Sitting Down to Think*, *Dressing up*, *On Winding Up the Clock* and *Other People's Games*. It is not surprising that he found himself unable to devise these essays side by side with writing narrative. So *Swallows and Amazons* had to be put aside and the articles continued to appear with

***Swallow*** and ***Amazon*** **by Roger Wardale**

Was Ransome's creative process similar to that of J.M. Barrie, who said that he had not focussed on the characteristics of any one boy, but rather that Peter Pan was concocted by rubbing the five Davies boys together, or were each of his characters based on a single person? John Walker, the eldest of the Swallows, was a steady, capable boy of whom Ransome's father would have approved. Throughout the series John's actions are shaped by a sense of duty and the standards he has been set by his father, a naval officer. Although he is protective of the younger members of the family, he is content to let Susan minister to their needs and happy to defer to Titty's romantic imagination. It is not clear where the name came from. Perhaps it was coincidence that John Walker was a well-known Bowness boatmen whose name was still to be seen over the door of one of the boat hirer's huts in the 1960s. The early notes for *Swallows and Amazons* were made in a Walker's loose-leaf binder. Walker was also the maiden name of his first wife.

Susan Walker took Susie Altounyan's name and her ability to handle *Swallow*, but several of those who remember Genia, including Susie herself, saw more than a passing resemblance to Ransome's own whistle-blowing mate and cook. Mate Susan is probably the least popular of the main characters and her acceptance of maternal and domestic responsibilities makes her almost unique in children's literature. Even Captain John accepts that he must fall in with her housekeeping arrangements. Captain Flint heaps praise upon her, and it is she who enables the Swallows to escape from parental care. She is also the focus for the Walkers as a family unit.

few breaks until the end of the year. He began to type the second draft on Boxing Day. The circumstances were hardly propitious, for he had fallen ill in Cairo while on his final trip abroad for the *Manchester Guardian*. Nevertheless when he returned to Ludderburn, he was able to press on with the revision which he completed by April. He visited Stephen Spurrier who was to illustrate the books. However, when Ransome saw the drawings, he rejected them out of hand and only the swashbuckling end-paper map was approved and that also featured as the dust jacket of the first edition.

Able-seaman Titty Walker has some of Titty Altounyan's characteristics and of course her 'rather silly' nickname. Possibly she was rubbed against Ransome's sister Joyce. The resulting spark was a bright one, for Titty Walker is one of Ransome's most original and best-loved characters. Among his papers is a note explaining the name: 'Titty is short for Tittymouse and Tittymouse is long for – it may be Ann or it may be Jane. I do not know; but as she is never known by any other name, it does not seem to matter. She was a very good Able Seaman.' Titty is an avid reader and a dreamer whose imagination links fantasy and reality. As Ernest Altounyan was quick to recognise, she is the real hero of *Swallows and Amazons*. The Boy Roger is likely to have been a similar mix of Roger Altounyan and Ransome's own younger brother Geoffrey. For the most part Roger is content to follow John and Titty, but he has a lively sense of fun and an independent streak, and refuses to accept the family view that motor boats are only engines in tin boxes.

The strongest evidence that Ransome recognised the Altounyans as originals is contained in a letter he wrote to his mother during a visit to Syria in 1932:

> ... but I must say it seems a little queer now after living with them all in S & A and Swallowdale, to meet them once more as actual human beings running about. My lot seem to me the solider, but Ernest's are very nice, and eager to know 'What is going to happen to us next?'

What of the Amazons? Ransome said that they sprung from a glimpse of two girls playing by the shore of the lake, one day while he was sailing on Coniston. Perhaps the two girls came from the days before the First World War when Ransome used to borrow *Jamrach*, or the first *Swallow*, from the Lanehead boathouse. Barbara and Dora Collingwood spring to mind, and it was to Barbara that Ransome once wrote for advice on sailing. Their mother (Edith Mary) was known in later life as Molly. In *Swallowdale*, Ransome says that the mother of the Amazons is called Molly. Was this just a coincidence? Whoever they were, the more intriguing puzzle is to try to discover if Captain Nancy Blackett, Terror of the Seas had an original? There has been more speculation about Nancy's creation than anyone's. It is here that the resemblance to Barrie's Peter Pan is strongest, for Nancy seems to be a combination of several strong-willed, imaginative girls Ransome had known, including Taqui Altounyan, whose letters to Ransome are very reminiscent of Nancy. W.G. Collingwood implied that Ruth-Nancy was his granddaughter Ruth, Robin Collingwood's child. She might seem a little young, having been born in 1921, but Ransome was having a huge game with people and places and we can only speculate.

Ransome's biographer, Hugh Brogan, saw a resemblance between Ransome's boyhood friend Ric Eddison and Nancy. Alternatively, Pauline Marshall, in her childhood memoir *How it all Began*, puts the case for herself and her elder sister Georgie being the original girls. They spent their holidays at Bank Ground and were a couple of spirited and adventurous tomboys and could have been the girls that Ransome had seen playing by the shore. Pauline recalls that following her first meeting with Ransome some time after publication, her father told her that they were the Amazons. The boisterous Nancy, setting the tune for everybody, is Ransome's most memorable creation. Her reputation for wildness is well-deserved, but from time to time there are glimpses of someone who is fiercely loyal to her family and friends and supportive of the younger ones, notably Titty and Dick. Peggy is simply the younger sister who is given to chattering in the early novels and whose very ordinariness makes her the ideal foil for Nancy.

Ransome wrote *Swallows and Amazons* for the Altounyans, to comfort them in what he saw as their exile, in return for the slippers. This is quite clear in the dedication. Originally he had settled on the num-

**Red cap sketches - by Evgenia Ransome?**

ber four, but changed his mind in order to include the parents. Brigit was still only three, and as he had said in his notes, did not count. It was intended to be a very personal gift in which the Altounyans could share his fun. Ransome hoped his friends would delight in the references and jokes that only insiders like themselves could understand. Nobody could have foreseen that the book would become famous and that it would be followed by eleven further stories which would bring sales of five million copies in the U.K. alone. Ransome could have had no idea that he would be besieged by questioners asking, 'Are they real?' Nobody could guess that the game would rebound on Altounyans and author alike, or that its origin would come under such scrutiny.

The Altounyans were delighted with their present and Dora immediately wrote to say they all liked it *enormously*. Ernest's response shows that he identified too closely with the Walkers. In a letter beginning 'Dear Captain Flint', he wrote: 'What I most especially like and marvel at is your extraordinary accurate characterisation of the kids. Each is just right – as far as I know them . . . Captain Flint is a very good *you* . . . I am personally quite content to go down to posterity as the author of the famous Duffer telegram. Dora is a little plaintive about her knowledge of kangaroos and what Bushie will say when she finds out that she has been libelled as Vicky I shudder to think'. He believed Taqui was Captain John and, for a while, that is how she signed her letters to Ransome. He was wrong about Mrs Walker, who was based on Ransome's own Australian mother, not Dora at all. The children understood that the book was really written for and not about them, but they all joined in Ransome's game, and Titty in particular seems to have tried to become like the able seaman so as to please Uncle Arthur. No matter who provided the starting point, all the characters owed more to Ransome's creative genius than they did to any living people.

Yet ever after that happy start, Ransome's gift has proved to be a mixed blessing. The characters seemed so real that readers who knew of the Altounyan involvement expected to find them like their fictional selves. When Taqui came to school in England she had to explain that she was not Captain John, and when the balletomane Susie Altounyan went to stay with school friends, she had to live down the 'Mate Susan' tag. Her hosts were quite relieved to find that, although she had lit fires and boiled kettles on Peel Island, she was not like Susan at all! As Taqui has said, 'We must have been pretty nearly the only children in England who did not spend our time playing Swallows and Amazons.'

Ransome's draft, *How Swallows and Amazons Came to be Written* continues:

> The book went on and on and grew bigger and bigger and instead of getting tired of it, I should have liked to be doing nothing else. I was enjoying my own childhood over again, all the best bits of it and the bits that might have been ever so much better if only something or other had been different. But then, as the book did at last come to an end (though there was no reason why I should have gone on for ever) I began to be very much afraid. For though the children in the book had taken things so much into their own hands that I could never be quite sure what they were going to do next, there they were, labelled with the names of the Walkers. And, oddly enough, I could not change their names, though it sounds so simple, just to go through the book with a pen and put new names in and cross out the old ones.

> As soon as I tried to change a name, there was a sort of revolt among the people in the book and nothing would go right. So there could be no possible pretending that the people in the book were not the people they actually were. There is a clause about libel between authors and publishers, and when I looked it up I did not like the look of it. Besides that, the Walkers were among my best friends, and I began to wonder what would have happened if they did not like their portraits, and still worse, if Captain John and Mate Susan and Able seaman Titty and the Boy Roger did not like theirs. And yet, I thought, even if the people outside the book don't like the people inside the book, the people inside have got some sort of right to be alive.'

He goes on to describe how 'Mr Walker' and his 'enormous family' came to the lake and sailed 'a regular fleet' of small boats including *Swallow* (there is no mention of *Mavis*). Ransome has clearly embroidered the truth a little. For example he says that the Walkers sent him a cable, whereas Dora Altounyan wrote within hours of receiving their copy of *Swallows and Amazons*.

Old friends sometimes quarrel and when, near the end of their lives Ransome and Altounyan had become irreconcilable, Ransome tried to suppress the Altounyan children's part in his story. Perhaps Altounyan had made too many claims on behalf of his family and implied that Ransome had simply taken his children as models, or perhaps Ransome was unconsciously jealous of a man who had succeeded in marrying a Collingwood. In a part of his *Autobiography* that was edited out of the published version after his death by Sir Rupert Hart-Davies, he wrote very differently:

> The children concerned are grown up now, some of them with children of their own, so that no feelings will be hurt if I tell the story of the mess into which I dived as a result of my benevolent but idiotic impulses. *Swal-*

*lows and Amazons* was already sketched out and the characters already named and living their own lives when, one day when I was working very hard, a car pulled up at Ludderburn and I saw Ernest Altounyan step out. I had already warned him that I was overwhelmed with work and for some days would have no time for visitors. I was very cross at seeing him and was moving towards the gate (wishing to forestall any invasion of the barn where all the tables were covered with sheets of my book) when it opened and two of the Altounyan children came through each holding out a red leather Arab slipper. My crossness ebbed away in a backwash of shame. I thought of those little Easterners going back to Aleppo and Syria, while the little English children of my book would be sailing in *Swallow* which I had allowed to remain on Coniston for a summer so that the little Altounyans should have two boats to play with. It occurred to me that it would be fun for the little Altounyans if I altered the names in my book so that they could at least pretend that the adventures in it were their own. It was not possible to take all their names, but I took three, Susan, Titty and Roger. My eldest was a boy, John, and I could not change him into a girl to match the eldest Altounyan, who was a girl called Taqui. But I did what I could, and, when the book was published and they read the dedication and remembered the incident of the slippers, they adopted my characters as their own and the generous-hearted Taqui said she did not at all mind being John. I had been a little afraid that their parents would object, but on the contrary, the time was to come when I had to answer an enquiry from Cambridge as to whether it was really true that Ernest Altounyan had sent the original of the telegram 'Better drowned than duffers if not duffers will not drown'. The whole family accepted responsibility for being the characters in my tale, though Dora did say that she did not understand why I had to give her an Australian grandmother.

The joke once started had to be kept up. I used to write to the Altounyans about 'our' children, and as for the children themselves it was clear that I must never, while they were children, deprive them of the 'selves'

they had so willingly adopted. This was all very well while they were in Syria, but was more than awkward in later years when it became difficult to reconcile, in the minds of people who knew both, these children of Aleppo, much of whose charm depended on their Eastern-ness with my four children who were just about as English as they could be. At first there was no difficulty for me because when I was writing *Swallows and Amazons*, I had hardly seen the Altounyan children half a dozen times and so had not been able to do more than borrow three of their names. It became more and more difficult when I had to deal with hordes of letters from other children asking 'Are they real?' and begging for their addresses, and with such letters as that of an American lady who wrote inviting me to bring (at her expense) the whole party of Swallows and Amazons over to America to spend the summer with her and her son. I had to find a formula that would not make my children less real for others than they were for me. I found one that served . . .' The only way to keep a secret (your own and other people's) is NEVER to answer a question.' I do not know yet what is the proper attitude in the presence of such questioners. My children were much more real to me than most of the people I knew. I had spent so much time with them. I knew so much more about them then ever I could put down on paper. It was a painful shock to be forced to remember that there are more kinds of reality than one. And it was made much worse when children wrote almost with indignation that they had met people who had told them that they were the Swallows and that they were not at all like the children in my books. I lamented many times that I had ever yielded to impulse and started of even helped the misunderstanding on its way.

No matter. Though the Altounyan children remarked, 'if you are writing about us, hadn't you better come and see us to find out what we are like?' they grew up in time, while all the adventures of my English family happened between 1929 and 1933, and with the increasing disparity in age the difficulty lessened, though I never got over the slight discomfort, when I met the little Easterners even when grown up and

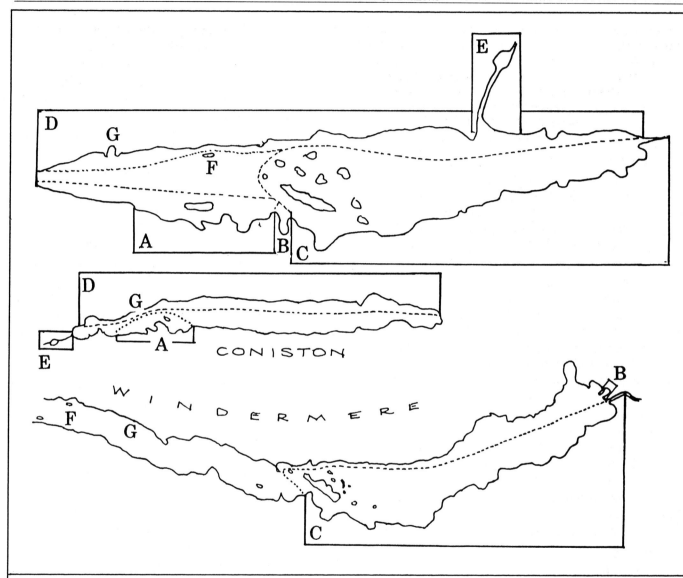

The Puzzle of Arthur Ransome's Lake – a possible solution

married, and always felt I had to protect *my* children against these very different people moving in a different world.

This version is neither supported by Ransome's notes in which Susan, Titty and Roger are the only names which remain unchanged, nor does it square with the entries in his diary. Nevertheless, it is hard not to sympathise with Ransome's difficulty in answering children's questions. Perhaps his reluctance to face their enquiries gave rise to his reputation for disliking children.

In *Swallows and Amazons* the Walker family stay at Holly Howe, a farm which was recognisable from the text as High Bank Ground Farm below Lanehead, even before Clifford Webb's drawing appeared in the second edition, and which Dora thought 'has quite a look of Bank Ground though wrong in almost every detail'. In the drafts for the story Ransome actually says Bank Ground and only at the last minute did he call the farm Holly Howe. The name comes from a large house to the north of Coniston village which today serves as a Youth Hostel. Holly Howe, like Bank Ground, lies above a field sloping down to some boathouses beside a lake. The lake is essentially Windermere, with additions from Coniston Water, and while many places are easily recognised, others have some degree of literary camouflage. Years later Ransome confided to Lady Liddell-Hart that one shore of his lake was Coniston and the other was Windermere, but it is more complicated than this.

While the children are waiting for permission from their absent father to borrow the sailing dinghy *Swallow* and camp on a nearby island, they look out from the Peak in Darien just as, some years before, Ransome had looked out from the rock at Reval (now Tallin) across the Baltic to the island of Nargon. The peak in Darien has been variously identified, but it

extends as the left-hand promontory of a very deep bay in which there is a boathouse. Just such a bay can be found at the head of Windermere and at its mouth is the little cliff known as Gale Naze Crag. When their father's telegram arrives giving permission, the Walkers (now the Swallows) set sail across uncharted waters. The lake has no ferry, but otherwise the life of Windermere, with its fishermen, steamers and racing yachts, is faithfully portrayed as a background to the children's games. The other lake users are regarded by the children as mere 'natives'.

On their voyage of discovery they are intrigued by a fat man living on a houseboat. At that time the *Esperance,* was moored in the bay south of Cockshot point on Windermere and used by Sir Samuel Scott's family as a houseboat. Stephen Spurrier's lively map decorated the end papers of *Swallows and Amazons* for many years, but his illustrations were heartily disliked by Ransome and never used. They do, however, confirm the identification by closely resembling photographs taken at the time. Years later Ransome admitted the connection, when he confessed to Sir Samuel's son, he had pulled alongside the houseboat and peeped through the windows!

Wild Cat Island with its steep, rocky sides and harbour is mostly Peel Island. W.G. Collingwood gave away this secret as long ago as 1932 in *The Lake Counties*. Anybody who has taken a boat into the hidden harbour on Peel Island, splashed ashore and scrambled over the rocks, needs little convincing that they have landed on Wild Cat Island. However, Ransome cooked up another juicy red herring by declaring in a letter that the island was Blake Holm on Windermere; an assertion perpetuated by Evgenia. Although *Swallows and Amazons* needed the impetus of the Altounyans, it is firmly rooted in Ransome's childhood holidays of a hundred years ago – and Peel Island was central to these memories.

Having spent their first night on the island, the explorers collect their milk from a conveniently situated nearby farm, just as Evgenia explained. Christina Hardyment in her jolly account of exploration and discovery, *Arthur Ransome and Captain Flint's Trunk* revealed how she had found a sketch-plan Ransome made of Dixon's Farm. From this she deduced it was based on Low Yewdale Farm, where he had stayed as a young man so as to be near the Collingwoods.

The Swallows spend the first few days fishing and gently settling in. Everything changes after the Amazons sail round the island flying the skull and cross-bones and soon the Swallows and Amazons have become allies and have embarked upon a war. The Amazons live at Beckfoot, a large, grey-stone house with a lawn leading down to a river shortly before it enters the lake. At the edge of the lawn is a boathouse bearing a painted skull and crossbones. Lanehead itself and Tent Lodge, a little further up the lake, are strong candidates, but neither are anywhere near a river, although Ransome's drawings do have a look of Tent Lodge. Just across the lake from Peel Island is a boathouse belonging to Oxen House, a large grey stone house that stands beside Torver Beck. It is possible that Ransome took the idea of a house beside a river from Oxen House and then moved the boat-house into the river itself to lead the Swallows towards the fun of Octopus lagoon. The Amazon River itself is Ransome's beloved Crake, and a quarter of a mile downstream is Octopus Lagoon masquerading under the name of Allan Tarn. Because Ransome wanted the Swallows to sail northwards on their cutting-out expedition to the Amazon River, the current is reversed so that the river flows into the lake.

After that famous first meeting of the Swallows and Amazons, it is the changing relationship between the Swallows and the houseboat man, now revealed as Nancy and Peggy's Uncle Jim, alias Captain Flint, which gives energy to the remainder of the book. At first the Swallows are suspected of putting a firework on the houseboat's roof and then they are accused of the burglary committed by a couple of local lads from Bigland on the night of the war with the Amazons, when Captain Flint's trunk is stolen. Reconciliation comes with Nancy's intervention and admission that it was she who burnt the cabin roof. Captain Flint finds himself in the Swallows debt when Titty discovers the stolen trunk on Cormorant Island.

Ransome tried several endings to the story. One interesting departure was to try writing a parallel narrative. After the burglary, Titty and Roger are allowed to row to Cormorant Island in search of the treasure. While they are away, Nancy gives Captain Flint the black spot and he follows her back to Wild Cat Island to make peace. Having found the trunk, Titty leaves Roger on guard while she delivers the news to the others and arrives to find the enemy seated in the camp.

Ransome readily identified Cormorant Island as Silver Holme on Windermere, and there seems no need to question it. Finally, after the storm washes out the island camp, the allies picnic in Horseshoe Cove. There are one or two possible coves on Windermere, which anyone who drifts along in a boat following Evgenia's advice can discover, but the most likely is Lazy Bay on the western shore, south of Grass Holme.

**Holly Howe.** *Roger, aged seven, and no longer the youngest of the family, ran in wide zigzags, to and fro, across the steep field that sloped up to Holly Howe, the farm where they were staying for part of the summer holidays.* **Swallows and Amazons**

**Wild Cat Island**. *And on the lake they had seen the island. All four of them had been filled with the same idea. It was not just **an** island. It was **the** island, waiting for them. It was **their** island.* **Swallows and Amazons**

**The Lake** . . . *the* Swallow *and her crew moved steadily southwards over a desolate ocean sailed for the first time by white seamen.* **Swallows and Amazons**

**Captain Flint's Houseboat in the 1930s.** *She was a long, narrow craft with a high raised cabin roof, and a row of glass windows along her side. Her bows were like the bows of an old-time clipper. Her stern was like that of a steamship. She had nothing that could properly be called a mast, though there was a little flagstaff, where a mast might have been, stepped just forward of the glass windowed cabin.* **Swallows and Amazons** (Photo: Sir Oliver Scott)

**The Camping Place.** *'Anyhow this is the best place for a camp,' said John. 'Let's put the tents up at once.'* **Swallows and Amazons**

**The Hidden Harbour**. *At last the green trees were close ahead, and* **Swallow** *was safe in the pool and ran her nose up the beach in a tiny bay, sheltered by trees from the north, and by the walls of rock from any other wind.* **Swallows and Amazons**

**Cormorant Island.** *There were plenty of other islands on the lake, but this was one they had not noticed, because it was very small, and so near the mainland that they had thought it was a promontory.* **Swallows and Amazons**

**Rio Bay**. *Three or four short tacks brought* Swallow *to the nearest of the landing stages for rowing boats that run out from the shore in Rio Bay.*
**Swallows and Amazons** (photo: Evgenia Ransome, courtesy Brotherton Library)

**Charcoal Burners' Wigwam.** *At the edge of the wood, not far from the smoking mound, there was a hut shaped like a round tent, but made not of canvas but of larch poles set up on end and all sloping together so that the longer poles crossed each other at the top.* **Swallows and Amazons**

**The River Amazon.** *Again there was a splash in the deep reed beds at the river's mouth. Again a duck quacked loudly. It quacked two or three times, until a voice said sternly, 'Stow it, you goat. Don't overdo things.'* **Swallows and Amazons**

**Horseshoe Cove**. '. . . *No one ever comes here except us, and no one can see we're here, even from the water, unless they happen to look right in.*'
**Swallows and Amazons**

# Chapter Three

# Developments and D.'s

No sooner was *Swallows and Amazons* in print, than Ransome was planning its successor. Furthermore, Cape told him not to waste time on anything else but to hurry on with the 'follow-up'. Ransome's response was to begin a version of *Peter Duck*, which he called *Their Own Story*. It was not long before he began to have second thoughts and in November 1930 confided to his mother that it would take a lot of working out and he doubted if he would be able to keep it up through 300 pages. The book was to be a combination of fictional fact (the Swallows and Amazons making up a story aboard a Norfolk wherry hired by Captain Flint for the winter holidays) and fictional fiction (their story of the *Wild Cat's* treasure-hunting voyage to the Caribbean). It was not long before he abandoned the attempt. His short draft was published in *Arthur Ransome and Captain Flint's Trunk* and, although it is an interesting false start, the mixture is not a happy one, and only serves to conform that he was right to do so.

Instead he returned to his fictional lake. As he explained to his young neighbour, Desmond Kelsall, the next book would be mostly land-based after Captain John becomes a little over-confident and wrecks *Swallow*. While he was writing *Swallows and Ama-* zons Ransome had slipped down to Barkbooth to read instalments to the Kelsalls and when he wanted the handwriting of a child for the Ship's Papers, Desmond and his brother Richard obliged by signing 'John Walker' and 'Roger'.

The news that Queen Mary had been to a well-known London bookshop and bought a copy of *Swallows and Amazons* gave Ransome further encouragement. He began the first draft of *Swallowdale* with relish on 3rd January 1931 and wrote in chronological order, with the plot clear in his mind. For once the story seems to have been constructed very quickly and Ransome set himself clear targets for the writing. By 18th January, he had completed 80 pages, but the diary gloomily records that he was 17 pages behind schedule. He took time off now and again for a little sailing and fishing until Clifford Webb's visit in April, by which time the first draft was nearly complete. Webb had been commissioned by Cape to illustrate the second edition of *Swallows and Amazons* as well as the new book, *Swallowdale*. Ransome took him in *Swallow* to Blake Holme and afterwards he sailed round and round while Webb sketched the little boat. Next day he took the artist aboard *Mavis* and sailed to Peel Island and then to the foot of Coniston Water. Ransome and Webb did not hit it off, but he had to admit that Webb's drawings were 'really v.g.'

There was a break from *Swallowdale* while the Ransomes hired a yacht on the Norfolk Broads. Then he began the revision and by July he was able to go to London with the finished typescript. Jonathan Cape's partner, G. Wren Howard liked the new book better than *Swallows and Amazons* and it was published in time for Christmas.

*Swallowdale*, even more than its predecessor, returns to the Lake District of his youth. It is Lake Country of hound trails, wrestling and village shows, in which the local farmers, woodmen and boat-builders are central. He permitted himself the luxury of allowing the plot to meander through more than 400 pages into which he put his love of the lakes in that lucid and economical style which was born of years of sending despatches from Russia.

The story begins when the Swallows keep their promise to return to Holly Howe. They set sail for the island where they find a message to say that Captain Flint and his nieces are housebound at Beckfoot, where they are entertaining Nancy and Peggy's Great Aunt. Next morning the Swallows sail to Horseshoe Cove to take up their exploration at the point where they had reached the previous summer. They are joined by Nancy and Peggy who have escaped in *Amazon* for a few hours. Horseshoe Cove in *Swallowdale* is rather more like one of the bays on the western shore at the southern end of Coniston Water than Lazy Bay on Windermere. When Titty and Roger have tired of listening to Nancy and Peggy's chatter, they decide to explore by following the beck which runs into the bay.

The landscape has lost the imaginative gloss of *Swallows and Amazons*, but Ransome's lyrical descriptions add greatly to the text:

The stream was too wide to jump across, but there were places where it was possible to hop from stone to stone and to get across with dry feet if you were lucky. The trees grew close to the stream, and in some places the water had hollowed out a way for itself almost under their roots. There were little pools, foaming at the top where the stream ran in, and smooth and shallow and fast at the hang before it galloped away again down a tiny cataract.

After going under the humpbacked bridge Titty and Roger continue to follow the beck upwards until they reach a waterfall at the foot of a secret valley. It is evident from Clifford Webb's illustration that he was taken to this waterfall, for his drawing is very precise. Swallowdale is to be found somewhere on Blawith Common. It has a Knickerbockerbreaker and an upper waterfall close at hand. Orienteering maps marking every waterfall show that there is only one valley with a pair of falls in this area. Of course Ransome embroidered it with literary camouflage, just as he had done with Wild Cat Island, and gave the valley an abandoned mine borrowed from elsewhere.

The following morning John wrecks *Swallow* on the Pike Rock at the entrance to Horseshoe Cove. Although they salvage her, and with the help of Captain Flint make her fit to sail to the boatyard in Rio Bay, she has to be repaired by boatbuilders. The boatyard is recognisable as Borwick's, which used to be situated at the south side of Bowness Bay. While she is being repaired, the Swallows have to move camp to the mainland and they settle in the secret valley Titty and Roger found. They are able to use the nearby Swainson's Farm for supplies and messages, and Mary Swainson darns Roger's shorts, just as Annie Swainson had done for young Arthur after he had spent a morning sliding down a nearby Knicker-bockerbreaker. In *Swallows and Amazons* a farm was merely a native settlement, but in *Swallowdale* it is given its own identity: the cart-track 'climbed away to the left and came out of the wood by an old white-washed farmhouse with a spring beside it and a stone trough, and a lot of ducks noisily enjoying the overflow from the trough'. The farm is not like Swainson's Farm at Nibthwaite, as the text and the head-piece (which was chosen from several different compositions) make clear.

While they are camping in Swallowdale, the Swallows catch fish in Trout Tarn a mile or so above the valley. This is Beacon Tarn which is about the right distance from the secret valley, but it is not linked by the beck mentioned in the book. Later they cross High Moor on their way to climb Kanchenjunga. Ransome accepted that Kanchenjunga was easily recognisable as The Old Man of Coniston and freely gave away that secret. It is not possible to identify High Moor so precisely, for there are several possibilities, but Little Arrow Moor is a strong candidate. They are guided towards the valley of the Amazon by four firs in a line. The Altounyans would have recognised these immediately, for the 'four firs' stood in the Lanehead garden.

After their noon-tide owl rendezvous with the Amazons, they row up the River Amazon, passing beneath not Yewdale Bridge at Coniston but Udal Bridge, until they reach the first cataract: 'a line of low waterfalls that marked the place where the mountain stream changed into the placid little river that wound through meadows to the lake'. At this point also the River Crake becomes Church Beck and the Swallows follow the Levers Water branch until they reach the campsite near to the place where the Low Water Beck joins Levers Water Beck. The following morning Nancy leads them across Levers Moss in the direction of the Pudding Stone, and then up the slope of Pudding Cove so as to cross the main path below Low Water before passing between the quarries to reach the summit from the east.

By now Great Aunt Maria has left and the Amazons are free to join the others in the camp at Swallowdale. Titty and Roger make their way back to Swallowdale by following an unlikely trail of pine cones across the moor, while the others cram into *Amazon*. Roger sprains an ankle and spends the night with the charcoal burners. This gives Ransome another opportunity to bring his old friends into the story to talk about traditional Lakeland wrestling and the Grasmere Sports.

*Swallow* is mended at last, but before they all return to Wild Cat Island, she defeats *Amazon* in a race from the houseboat to the Beckfoot boathouse. The book ends with Susan once more attending to the fire on Wild Cat Island and exclaiming, 'Isn't it a blessing to get home?'

There were more rounds of applause from Aleppo and urgent requests for the Ransomes to visit them in Syria to see how the children are growing up. Early in 1932 they went, partly to satisfy these demands and also to take them a little sailing dinghy. Besides, Earnest Altounyan was convinced that he could cure Ransome's stomach problems which had defeated his Harley Street specialist. He was not successful, but Ransome was able to make good progress with *Peter Duck*. On their return Evgenia travelled ahead while Ransome visited Lowestoft to check the accuracy of the opening chapters of the new book. When she arrived home she found that the house had been burgled, and by the time Ransome arrived she was dealing with the burglary in her masterful fashion leaving him to get on with his revision.

Cape wanted Ransome to illustrate the book himself. Perhaps they had endured enough of his strong disapproval of the work of Stephen Spurrier and Clifford Webb. Figures bothered Ransome so much that he tried using live models whom he could photograph so that he could work from the prints. Colonel Kelsall joined in the fun and constructed a capstan and bunk beds. His two sons Richard and Desmond were the models, together with Peggy and Joan Hudson from Bowness. Ransome thought them 'v. jolly infants' and called the photographs 'Hollywoods'. Sometimes of a winter evening he would invite the children to a party in the workroom, where he would issue his guests with penny whistles and fetch out his accordion so that they could sing sea shanties.

Developing the characters of Captain Flint, Peter Duck (based on Carl Sehmel, his crew aboard *Racundra*) and the red-haired boy gave him some fun, but unlike the writing of *Swallows and Amazons*, he had to struggle to complete the book in time for publication before Christmas. Perhaps he was already beginning to tire of his Swallows and Amazons. He did not sail *Swallow* until July. At the end of August the Altounyans returned to Lanehead shortly before the four eldest children were due to start school in England. In September they were all to have raced, but Evgenia noted in her diary: 'Joined in the "all-comers" and last of the season' race on Windermere. Ernest was to have raced Shepherd's *Bittern*, but somehow or other muddled it up and did not get the boat, but took the children on to the ferry landing to watch miserably us sailing THEIR *Swallow*. It was squally and wet and the mast cracked with a loud noise. We hadn't quite completed the first round when the winner passed the finishing line. We got soaked to the skin but it was most enjoyable sailing.' The year ended on a happy note with the news that *Peter Duck* had been reprinted. 'We shall pull through!' Ransome told his mother.

Memories of the Great Frost of 1895 and the more recent one of 1929 gave Ransome inspiration for his next book. Furthermore, he had the brilliant idea of seeing the hard winter and the established characters from the viewpoint of two newcomers. We meet the academic Dick and the literary Dorothea Callum, who are London children of a professor of archeology. In many ways Dick is Arthur himself, a bespectacled young scientist fascinated with natural history, astronomy, chemistry or whatever took his fancy. Similarly Dick's habit of carrying a pocket book with him everywhere came from Ransome, who started a fresh one each year. Two entries will be familiar to readers of *Winter Holiday*; the first from 1929: 'Light = 186,000 miles per second', and the other from 1930: 'Mumps from contact 29 days'. This time Ransome must have felt free to borrow the name Dick from Ted Scott's son who survived the boating tragedy which had killed his father on Windermere the previous year. There is a temptation to associate the name with Dick Kelsall, but Ransome, writing in his diaries and elsewhere, called him Richard. Dorothea probably came from Dora (Dorothy) Collingwood. There is a reason for supposing that Ransome had his sister Joyce in mind, for she also wrote stories in little notebooks and later children's books. Dorothea lacks Titty's self confidence, and for much of the time is content to be a follower of others. Only in *The Big Six* does she take the lead in piecing together the evidence which leads to George Owden's downfall. In the three final Lake District novels, by allowing the reader to share Dorothea's viewpoint, Ransome creates some of his most effective images.

Ransome began *Winter Holiday* early in 1933, but its execution gave him any amount of anguish and trouble and he bothered himself about what readers would say when they found that the Swallows and Amazons were not the central characters. 'I doubt if Dorothea and Dick fit this strange tale', he entered in his diary. He poured out his troubles to his publishers, to whom he described the unfinished text in one word: 'Bilge'. 'Book no good and will not be done,' he lamented, while to his mother, he wrote, 'Cape insists on me doing my own pictures. Hell!!!'

It is the week after Christmas and Dick and Dorothea are staying at Dixon's Farm. On their first morning the newcomers see the Swallows and Amazons on the island and in the afternoon, while they are looking for somewhere for Dick to do his star-gazing, they see them again at Holly Howe. Dick suggests signalling, but it is Dorothea who pushes him into actually carrying it out after nightfall. Eventually their signals are seen and this leads to a meeting the following morning.

Nancy, with typical generosity of spirit, is impressed with the signalling idea and invites them to join in the latest game which takes the form of a North Polar Expedition. When it is discovered that the newcomers are excellent skaters they are not merely tolerated but welcomed. The Swallows have everything to learn about skating, and a delightful passage in the book came from the Altounyan girls, who were at Annisgarth School in Windermere, learning to skate on Tarn Hows that winter. They used to visit Low Ludderburn at weekends, sometimes staying for a day or two, and were treated to readings of work in hand and occasionally taken sailing.

The barn above Dixon's Farm becomes a signal station so that the D.'s can receive messages from Holly Howe and join the others each day. The signals were already in use between Low Ludderburn and the barn at Colonel Kelsall's home at Barkbooth. In their final form they could convey 74 messages. Mostly the elaborate system was intended for fishing messages, but without leaving the terrace in front of the cottage Evgenia could arrange for the colonel to collect her at a certain time and take her shopping in Windermere.

The signals were invaluable on one occasion when Ransome fell ill and Kelsall arrived at the cottage a quarter of an hour after Evgenia had hoisted her S.O.S.

When it is discovered that Nancy has mumps, there is general rejoicing that the others will have an extra month's holiday. Ransome paints a delightful picture of Windermere during one of those rare winters when the lake freezes from end to end. The Arctic explorers are able to camp each day in the houseboat in its new role as the *Fram*, originally the vessel of the Norwegian Arctic explorer Nansen, whom Ransome had met. Captain Flint returns and meets the D.'s in one of the most amusing episodes in the series. He is invited to join the expedition's march to the head of the lake to discover the North Pole. The D.'s are overtaken by a blizzard and their sailing sledge is blown to the head of the lake before crashing on the shore. They manage to reach the summer-house which Captain Flint has borrowed for the North Pole and the others eventually follow with their relief expeditions.

There has been almost as much speculation about the origin of the North Pole as there has about Swallowdale. People have 'remembered' it at various places and until recently the conservatory extension to Wanless Howe, just above the road running by Borrans Park (which I photographed in the 1960s), had seemed the most likely. Then Dick Kelsall remembered he had seen the very summer-house in the exact spot at the head of the lake around 1930. A local member of the Arthur Ransome Society, Jim Andrews, confirmed this by dowsing and even found the bow windows of which Ransome spoke. I have seen a demonstration of this dowsing, and most impressive it is too, for there are a lot of Roman remains in the area to which the dowsing rods also respond. I

**Through the Snow** (from **Winter Holiday**)

**Captain Nancy gives instructions** (from **Winter Holiday**)

have tried without success to find supporting evidence for their find. No photographs, maps or land use surveys that I have studied make any reference to a building at that particular spot. Nor do any of the Waterhead residents questioned remember any building in the field – and one person's memory went back to 1922. The land belonged to Ambleside Urban District Council, having been purchased by public subscription in 1925. There was however a flagpole at the Wateredge Hotel where the Ransomes used to go for tea. Until further support is available, it still seems more likely that the old conservatory at Wanlass Howe, high above the road, was the inspiration. It fits the two finished drawings in *Winter Holiday* which show the building above the explorers and not on the almost flat ground of Borrans Park.

All through a very hot summer Ransome wrestled with his winter story which – unlikely as it seems when one reads it now – would not come right for him: 'blessed if I know what's wrong with it, but I know jolly well something is,' he wrote to Wren Howard on 22nd August after first the beginning and then the end had given him sleepless nights. 'For goodness sake, have a look at the proofs when they come along.' By the end of the month the script had gone off direct to Greys, the printers, presumably before anyone at Cape had read or edited it. Ransome enclosed details of the spaces to be left for the pictures over which he continued to sweat. 'John is my trouble,' he wrote to Wren Howard on 25th. 'In two of my best drawings he has turned into a clumsy lout of seventeen or eighteen. I can't keep him young.'

It is not hard to imagine the panic, with his publisher banking on finished copies of the book in time to get them into the shops for pre-Christmas sales. By mid-September Ransome had begun to cheer up, principally due to a good, if not wholly uncritical, report from Wren Howard. 'I am most awfully pleased that you like *Winter Holiday*,' he replied to Howard's praises. 'I felt so hopeless about it for so long that I was sure everybody would feel the same.' After answering questions about the incubation period of mumps and confessing to an error in the semaphore alphabet, he invited his publisher in a 'P.S.' to 'Throw out ANY or ALL of course'.

By the beginning of December, it was all smiles again. The book sold 1500 copies on the day of publication and its author was blushing with embarrassment at his publisher's support. 'I say, you really are going it,' he wrote to Wren Howard on 3rd December. 'Today's advertisement in the *Observer* is something tremendous. I couldn't believe it referred to me . . . turned pinker than ever when I saw it.' All the anguish – for the moment – evaporated in a success that outstripped both *Swallows and Amazons* and *Swallowdale*.

The euphoria was shortlived, for another struggle began when he moved the D.'s to the Norfolk Broads for his next book, *Coot Club*, which arose out of Ransome's own sailing there in 1933 and 1934. A new set of characters and a new environment didn't come easy to him, but his story of bird protection in the teeth of aggressive carelessness on the part of the visiting Hullabaloos. who hunt down the young conservationists with their noisy motor cruiser, rings as true today as it did in the 1930s.

For his next book he returned to the Lake District and another land-based adventure. An entry in his diary for 1929 noted that Oscar Gnosspelius had found copper on Coniston Old Man. Gnosspelius was an old family friend who had married Barbara Collingwood after a varied career which included civil engineering in Africa and South America and various forms of aero engineering (he designed and built a float plane that took off from Lake Windermere). They settled at High Hollin Bank, a little distance from Lanehead. Copper had been mined in the Coniston fells for over three hundred years, but since the beginning of the century attempts to find economically workable copper veins had been sporadic and short-lived. This one was similarly unsuccessful, and by the time Ransome was writing *Pigeon Post* it had been abandoned.

The story starts at the beginning of the following summer holidays. Titty and Roger arrive by train at Strickland Junction, easily recognisable from the text as Oxenholme, but disguised by the mirror-drawing used as a frontispiece. Here they find a pigeon basket awaiting their collection. After releasing the pigeon, they continue their journey to Windermere where they are met by Nancy and her mother in Rattletrap. Almost certainly, this was based Ransome's open Trojan car which he had been driving for a while. They arrive at Beckfoot to find the Swallows, Amazons and D.'s camping in the Beckfoot garden. This is because Mrs Blackett wants to keep them within reach until Mrs Walker comes to Holly Howe and they can return to Wild Cat Island. Much to Nancy's disgust. Captain Flint has gone to South America on a mining trip. She decides that if they could find gold in the fells, he would not go gallivanting off just when she wants him aboard the houseboat to join in her games. She takes them all up the Amazon River and part way up Kanchenjunga into a tunnel where an old miner, Slater Bob, confirms that there is gold to be found in the fells.

Slater Bob was John (Willie) Shaw and the mine, known as Horse Crag Level, is at Tilberthwaite, not far from the bridge. The mine is just as Ransome described it, with a long tunnel leading to a chamber which was built originally as a drain for the copper mine and reopened for slate – much what Slater Bob told the prospectors. When Oscar Gnosspelius abandoned his attempt to mine for copper in 1933 he set up Shaw at Horse Crag Level, and there he remained until he retired in 1938.

Old Bob tells them of gold that is to be found somewhere on the other side of the mountain, much to the consternation of Mrs Blackett who does not want them charging around all over the country while there is such a high risk of fell fires at the end of a long hot summer. Eventually, after they arrange to camp beside a farm at the head of

**Beckfoot sketch by Arthur Ransome**

**Slater Bob talks of gold** (from **Pigeon Post**)

the valley and send a pigeon with a message every day to say that they are all well, she capitulates. The ingenious contrivance by which the pigeons are made to ring a bell in the Beckfoot hall as they enter the pigeon loft across the stable yard was the work of Dick Kelsall. He and his brother and the Hudson girls helped Ransome with some more Hollywoods for the illustrations which he was now expected to provide.

Having left the gear at the farm with Mrs Tyson, they climb the steep track to the gold fields which Ransome called High Topps. This country has been cleverly disguised by creating it in the mirror image of reality. Yewdale Beck above Shepherd's Bridge is the upper reaches of the River Amazon with its winding, undulating road and a bridge over the beck at Tilberthwaite leading to a farm. To the south of the beck is the high rocky plateau under the shoulder of Weatherlam which Ransome chose for his gold fields. It is confirmed by a diary entry for 27th March 1935 when he went up behind Tilberthwaite with 'Gnossie', to see several of the old copper workings and 'a suitable bit of country for my story'. Gnosspelius showed Ransome the proper way to pan for gold and how to use a blowpipe – skills essential to the development of the story.

When Titty finds water by dowsing in an old charcoal burner's pitstead on the edge of High Topps they can all move nearer to their work. A stranger, whom the prospectors call Squashy Hat, is suspected of being a rival as he studies his map and paints white spots marking a vein of copper on the slopes. Squashy Hat was based on Gnosspelius himself. Eventually Roger discovers the gold while indulging in a private game and John and Nancy insist on proper crushing and panning in order that Captain Flint may be greeted with a nugget of pure gold on his return. The younger ones are instructed to watch Squashy Hat. They become trapped in a tunnel from which their rival has just emerged when 'The Old Level' collapses behind them. Thanks to Dick's good sense and cool head, they are able to escape through the mountain to Slater Bob's. It was once possible to go from High Topps to Slater Bob's in reality, but as it involved a descent of 500 feet, it was not just a simple matter of walking along tunnels. In June Gnosspelius was helping again, demonstrating crushing and panning and finally taking Ransome up Swallow Scar and Wetherlam. It was 'very jolly up there above the screes', wrote Ransome, who watched peregrine falcons.

The blast furnace is a disaster and the young prospectors are almost burnt by a fell fire before Captain Flint returns at last and they discover that what they have found is a rich vein of copper. This

**Sketch of an unknown worker with a pestle and mortar** (by Arthur Ransome)

**Nancy crushing the gold dust** (from **Pigeon Post**)

turns out to be exactly what Captain Flint and his shy friend, the rival prospector who had returned early, had been looking for all the time.

Once again Ransome was having a hard time with the writing and he wrote gloomily: ' . . . read it all through. AWFUL. No grip anywhere. Masses of corroborating detail needed & no *tension*.' And again: 'The whole book is somehow not there . . . all but lifeless. I can't *think* of it'. Reading the beautifully constructed plot with its parallel climax and wealth of detail, it is difficult to imagine how much it cost its author, but perhaps things were never so bad as they seemed. He was slow with the illustrations too, due perhaps to spending too much time aboard his sea-going boat, *Nancy Blackett*. His publisher chased him for them, and it was again the end of August before *Pigeon Post* could go ahead at the printers.

Many readers believe Ransome's story of the Swallows' accidental voyage across the North Sea to be his best, but it pleased him little more than the others when finished. 'I am very dissatisfied with parts of it,' he wrote to Wren Howard, when sending him *We Didn't Mean to Go to Sea*, 'I fear a lot of people will say the thing's too tough for babes.'

*We Didn't Mean to Go to Sea* was followed by *Secret Water*, which examines the conflict between following personal inclinations and being loyal to one's friends. The ninth book in the series, and the fourth with an East Anglian setting, was a thrilling detective story, *The Big Six*. Then came a sequel to the Peter Duck fantasy, *Missee Lee*, set in China. Not until they were living beside Coniston Water during the Second World War, did Ransome return to his lake country for the last time.

*The Picts and the Martyrs* is the shortest of the entire canon and it brought forth the fiercest criticism from Evgenia. In August 1941 he had written a letter to Margaret Renold explaining his idea of the Great Aunt's unwelcome visit to Beckfoot while Nancy and Peggy are in charge during their mother's absence. The following March he confided. 'I wish I had another wild Peter Duck or Missee Lee plot. The new book with strictly domestic interest is damnable. I hate it and so will everyone else.'

By August it was finished and Ransome fled to Hampshire where he spent the weekend fishing while Evgenia read it. She hated it. 'Anything is better than to have a book to your name of which you are ashamed . . . Your rivals would be very happy and well justified in saying that you "missed the bus" . . . She was wrong in her poor opinion of the book and wrong in trying to bully Arthur into discarding it. Ransome revised the manuscript briefly. He did not send the final script to Cape until after he had shown it to his mother in December. She liked it, and this gave Ransome the moral support he needed to face up to Evgenia's hostility. Desperately he set to work on the illustrations and *The Picts and the Martyrs* – perhaps the funniest of all his books – was published in June 1943 to a warm welcome from all his readers who delighted in the return to the familiar Lakeland scene.

The story opens at the beginning of the summer holidays with Nancy and Peggy alone at Beckfoot while their mother recuperates from an illness. Captain Flint has taken her on a cruise which somehow the Great Aunt comes to hear about and decides it is her duty to take over the household. To make matters worse, the D.'s have just arrived. Nancy realises that the G.A. thinks her mother is being irresponsible and will be even more cross with her if she finds that they have been allowed to have visitors. The only solution is for the D.'s to lie hid for the duration of her visit in an old hut called The Dogs' Home in the nearby woods. There is just such a hut among the Forestry Commission woodlands north of Ransome's old home at The Heald. The name has puzzled a number of people, but among the end-paper advertisements in the diary which Ransome bought each year, there is the Battersea Dogs' Home panel, headed boldly 'The Dogs' Home'.

To complicate matters, the D.'s are expecting to sail their new boat which they have named *Scarab* after the sacred beetle of the ancient Egyptians. *Scarab* was based on his own dinghy, *Coch-y-bonddhu*. Dick is also to help with the analysis of the copper samples from the mine which Captain Flint's partner, Timothy, hopes to complete before his return. Dorothea has to learn housekeeping and Dick has to master sailing in order to do everything they had planned and yet remain hidden for almost a fortnight. In the end Nancy's plan succeeds in spite of complications caused by Dick's 'burglary' of Beckfoot and the Great Aunt's fixation that the Swallows are around somewhere.

*The Picts and the Martyrs* is the ultimate development of Ransome's fictional Lake District. The local folk are not regarded as quaint exotics labelled 'savages', as they had been by the imaginative Titty in *Swallows and Amazons*, but have become three-dimensional and as much a part of the scene as the great hills. Ever since their arrival at Dixon's Farm in *Winter Holiday*, the D.'s have related to the local people in a way the Swallows, except Roger with old Mr Swainson, have not. In *The Picts and the Martyrs*, Jacky the farm boy is central to their successful survival in the hut in the wood and a reminder that Ransome himself had learnt from the country people in his youth and during his boyhood holidays at Nibthwaite. On the night of her arrival, Dorothea's response: 'There isn't a lovelier place in all the world,' sets the tone for the book which became Ransome's final expression of his love affair with the Lake District of his youth and its most complete evocation.

For a dozen years he had been storing up the idea for a Victorian tale about 'an old schoolmaster and a fisherman and a boy and a river', a *Bevis*-like novel based on Tom Stainton, the water bailiff of the River Beela. He called it *The River Comes First* and wrote several chapters of narrative and, despite greatly improving it when he abandoned the attempt to tell it in the first person, he finally gave up. Evgenia's strong opposition must have had some bearing on the decision, but what he did write shows that Ransome's power of imagery was undiminished:

The gamekeeper's cottage stood where it stands today set back in the edge of the wood and looking out over the straight bit of the river that is known as Long Dub. Some of the trees have grown since then, but others have been cut, and probably it was then much as it is now, sheltered by the wood from the south-west wind and catching the morning sun across the river. It was a two-storied cottage, rough cast and white-washed, with a slate-roofed porch covered with a climbing rose that had been planted on the gamekeeper's wedding day, a present to Tom's mother from the old gardener at the hall. In fourteen years it had covered the porch and was spreading over the side of the house, all but framing the window of the kitchen. It was one of those roses that find it hard to make up their minds to stop flowering, and it was Mary Staunton's pride that in all but the hardest winters she was able to pick a bud from it, and have it blossom in the house on Christmas Day. Inside the porch, over the door, there was nailed the antler of a deer, from which hung an old cowbell, with a string to the clapper of it and a fox's pad to the end of that, a handle for anybody who wanted to ring the bell.

Similarly in this description of the river during a drought:

The river was dead low, stones showing that I'd never seen above water, moss on the flats and hardly a stir in the pools. You could see the fish crossing the shallows with their back fins out . . . Fainting hot it was, with no wind and never a stir in the reflections but for a trout. Looking up the river, you could see every tree and leaf in the water above the ford, and looking across to the wood it was the same and the sun coming off the water like a warming pan held to your face.

Ransome tried to bring his Norfolk boys – central characters in *Coot Club* and *The Big Six* – to visit the D.'s and their friends on the lake in the unfinished story that Hugh Brogan discovered while researching his *Life of Arthur Ransome*. It had no title and Brogan called it *Coots in the North*. It was finally published in 1988, together with a number of other Ransome short stories, including two brilliant self-contained passages from *The River Comes First*. After Joe, Bill and Pete have stowed away on board a cruiser being transported to Rio, and they have met Nancy and Peggy clowning about on the lake, the story peters out, although Ransome left a clear outline for the remainder of the book.

He took the setting of his fishing holidays in the Hebrides for the last of the series, *Great Northern?* The plot was suggested by his friend, Myles North and brought the Swallows, Amazons and D.'s into conflict with a determined, but eventually unsuccessful egg collector intent on stealing the eggs of the first great northern diver to nest in Britain. *Great Northern?* is best enjoyed as a fantasy like *Peter Duck* and *Missee Lee*. This time the Swallows and Amazons have been joined by Dick, who suggested the story, and Dorothea who played a large part in its creation.

The series properly reaches its conclusion at the end of *The Picts and The Martyrs* with the Swallows due to arrive and Nancy, about to hoist the skull and crossbones on the Beckfoot promontory, reminding everyone that there are '. . . five whole weeks of the holiday still to go.'

**ook Out Point.** *For a long time after breakfast was over and washing up done they kept watch on Look Out Point for the coming of the Amazon.*
*wallowdale*

**Horseshoe Cove.** *At the very end of the northern of the two headlands that made the narrow entrance to the cove, a large towel was waving on the top of an oar fixed in the rocks.* **Swallowdale**

**Rio Boatbuilders.** *All along this nearer side of Rio Bay were the building yards, where rowing boats were built, and little ships like Swallow, and racing yachts, besides motor boats for the people who did not know how to manage sails. There were boathouses and little docks. There were sheds a few yards back from the water, with railway lines running down into the lake, and wheeled carriages resting on the railway lines to carry boats down into the water and to bring them up out of it.* **Swallowdale**

**Swallowdale Waterfall.** *They hurried on until they stood below the waterfall. Above them the water poured noisily from ledge to ledge of rock, and they could get no further without climbing up the rocks beside the falling water ...* **Swallowdale**

**The Top Waterfall, Swallowdale.** *'I'm going to dam the top pool for one thing,' said John, 'to make a bathing place.'* **Swallowdale**

**Swallowdale.** *It was a little valley in the moorland, shut in by another waterfall at the head of it, not a hundred yards away . . .* **Swallowdale**

**Trout Tarn**. *Trout Tarn was nearly a mile beyond Swallowdale, high on the top of the moor, a little lake lying in a hollow of rock and heather. When the Swallows saw it, they wished almost that they had made their camp on its rocky shores.* **Swallowdale**

**Octopus Lagoon.** *'Here's the lagoon.' said Susan, and the boat shot out into a small lake almost covered by big patches of broad-leaved water-lilies. Even in daylight it was hard not to catch them with the oars.* **Swallowdale**

**Kanchenjunga Beck**. *The stream hurrying down from Kanchenjunga fell far more steeply then the little beck that had led the able-seaman and the boy to the discovery of Swallowdale. It dropped sometimes ten, twenty feet at a time into pools from which the white foam spurted high in air to meet it.* **Swallowdale**

**The Half-way Camp.** *To the left the peak of Kanchenjunga rose above the lesser crags that curved about the head of the ravine. Far up among those they could see thin white lines where the becks were still carrying water collected on the tops. To right and left were the rough fells through which it seemed that the little stream at their feet had carved a channel fit for a river a thousand times bigger than itself.* **Swallowdale**

**Kanchenjunga Summit**. *Then indeed they knew that they were on the roof of the world.* **Swallowdale**

**View from the Summit.** *'And there's Scawfell . . .'* **Swallowdale**

**Dixon's Farm.** *Dick and Dorothea came round the corner of the house and out into the road between the garden and a huge barn.* **Winter Holiday**

**The Igloo.** . . . *at the back of this platform, nestling against the hill, was a low hut with no windows, looking almost like a heap of stones.*
**Winter Holiday**

**Rio.** *'Well, he's simply disappeared,' said Titty. 'Gone through a hole in the ice. said Roger cheerfully. But just then they saw him coming down out of the village, towing his sledge behind him.* **Winter Holiday**

**io Bay, 1929.** *Rio bay was this morning more crowded than ever. It was as if everybody was afraid the weather was going to break, and was taking last chance on the ice.* **Winter Holiday** (Photo: Arthur Ransome, courtesy Brotherton Library)

**The North Pole?** *It was queerly shaped and could hardly have been called a house. The end of it that was nearest to them seemed to be nearly all glass, like a bow window, a big bow window, with snow crusted on the panes. It was only one storey high.* **Winter Holiday**

**Slater Bob's Mine**. *'There it is,' said Nancy at last, and pointed ahead of them, up the side of the Scar to a rampart of loose stones that rose out of the heather and bracken and scorched grass. 'All that stuff has come out of the inside of the hill.'* **Pigeon Post**

**The Entrance to Slater Bob's Mine.** *And then turning a corner between high walls built up on either side of then, they saw a narrow railway line disappear into a black hole in the rock.* **Pigeon Post** (Photo: Ted Alexander)

**Inside Slater Bob's.** *They were at the mouth of a lofty chamber in the rock. The dazzling light of the acetylene lamp, that hung from an iron spike driven into a crack in the rock, showed them a short, broad-shouldered old man leaning on a baulk of timber that he had been shaping with an axe.*
**Pigeon Post** (Photo: Ted Alexander)

**The Amazon River.** *Their own road was narrow and winding, going up the valley close to the dried-up little river.* **Pigeon Post**

**High Topps.** *'Well, what do you think of it?' said Nancy, waving her arm as if she had somehow herself conjured the whole of High Topps into existence.* **Pigeon Post**

**The Dogs' Home.** *'That old place,' said Cook. 'There's no glass in the window and the roof's likely enough down by now.'* **The Picts and the Martyrs**

**Grey Screes**. *All afternoon Squashy Hat was moving slowly about on the steep slopes of Grey Screes.* **Pigeon Post**

**The Dogs' Home**. *'Of course anybody could get in at the window if they wanted said Dorothea.* **The Picts and the Martyrs**

**The Tern**. *The steamer, with a great flurry of reversed propellers, was coming alongside the pier.* **The Picts and the Martyrs**

'The Explorers' sketch by Arthur Ransome

The Explorers (from Swallowdale)

# Chapter Four

# Following the Ransome Trail

When trying to find exact locations for Ransome's stories explorers should not be influenced by his illustrations, for these do not always represent the text. The drawing 'The Camp Fire' in *Swallows and Amazons*, for example, shows an open space between the camp and the landing place. *Swallow* is clearly visible, yet we are told that the camp is surrounded by trees. Ransome changed his sketch of Titty and Roger paddling beneath the bridge on their way to the discovery of Swallowdale in order to make the figures larger. In doing so he had to alter the shape of the bridge.

The profusion of locations that might have been in Ransome's mind when he created his Lakeland geography, adds to the difficulty in pin-pointing exact spots. If you explore the shores of Windermere and Coniston Water you will find several possible Dariens and bays reminiscent of Horseshoe Cove. Perhaps the closest we shall come to finding the key to unlock Ransome's secrets is by trying to visualise how well, and in what circumstances, he was likely to have known each place.

Writing in the *Junior Bookshelf* journal in 1936, Arthur Ransome explains:

The country is the country of my own childhood . . . Then there has to be a little pulling about of rivers and roads, but every single place in those books exists somewhere and by now I know the geography of the country in the books so well that when I walk about in actual fact, it sometimes seems to me as if some giant or earthquake has been doing a little scene shifting overnight.

Pilgrims on the Ransome trail today will be more likely to be stuck in a queue along the A591, than rattling along the single railway line to Windermere. The tiny modern station is not even the same elegant Victorian train hall which was 'nearly filled' by the Ransomes and the Gnosspelius family when they met the Altounyans arriving from Syria in 1932. This is now a supermarket. Nevertheless, as the road reaches the top of the final rise above the station, the view is much the same as that which greeted Titty and Roger arriving by train in *Pigeon Post*. The sparkling water of Windermere stretches into the distance, and beyond the trees on the other side of the lake are the distant mountains. The town of Windermere is not Rio. That honour belongs to Bowness, its neighbour, a mile or so to the south-west. The town of Windermere was built in the middle of the nineteenth century, within a few years of the completion of the railhead in 1847, and this accounts for the similarity of the confident grey-stone buildings that give the place a feeling of unity and solidarity. The Terrace still stands above the station, and looks much the same as it did when Arthur's Aunt Susan lived there and gave him Sunday lunches during his time at The Old College.

St Mary's Church, where the boys from The Old College worshipped, stands not far away towards the northern end of the town. The Old College itself was nearby at the end of Old College Lane. The footpath along which Ransome dawdled listening to the music of the beck when going on a school walk, is probably the Sheriff's Walk footpath which leaves the road to Bowness after about three-quarters of a mile at Goody Dale. The path leads through a wood, past an unexpected waterfall and reaches the road by the lake near to the Windermere Steamboat Museum.

The museum has a unique collection of Victorian steam yachts and among them, tied up to the jetty, is a craft that enthusiasts will quickly recognise as Captain Flint's houseboat. Her long, narrow hull with its clipper bow, counter stern and high elegant cabin roof make her unmistakable. Apart from her role in *Swallows and Amazons, Esperance* is notable as the oldest twin-screw craft in the world and also the most venerable vessel in Lloyds Register of Yachts, having been built in 1869, the same year as *Cutty Sark*. She was constructed from the finest iron for H.W. Schneider, who was himself an iron magnate, in order to take him on his daily journey from his pier in Bowness Bay to Lakeside where his personal train took him to Barrow and his ironworks. Schneider lived at Belsfield, the large house overlooking Bowness Bay and had so many servants looking after his needs that he built two terraces in Bowness to house them.

Also on display in the museum (and on permanent loan) is *Mavis* which was sailed by various members of the Altounyan family until the death of Roger Altounyan in 1988. She has been fully restored following Christina Hardyment's rallying cry to which hundreds responded with upwards of £3,000 in donations. *Mavis* was renamed *Amazon* at the inaugural meeting of The Arthur Ransome Society in 1990 and most people believe that she was the original *Amazon*. It must be conceded, however, that while Ransome's dinghy *Swallow* in the story *Swallows and Amazons* was accurately described in every detail, *Amazon* was almost new and had varnished planking, while *Mavis* was not new and had almost certainly never been varnished. Sadly, there is no hope of the museum being able to display *Swallow* as she has not survived the passage of time. When Ransome left the Lake District in 1935, *Swallow* was bought by Roger Fothergill, a young Swallows and Amazon enthusiast, who continued to sail on Windermere until the start of the Second World War. After that time, neither I nor anyone else has been able to find out anything definite, although there has been a rumour that *Swallow* ended her days as a maritime flower-pot in a Windermere garden.

Ransome chose well when he gave the village of Bowness the name Rio, for in the high season there is dancing on the foreshore and the constant stream of visitors coming and going make it is as crowded as any Rio carnival. Unfortunately, the chemist's shop that had a sudden run on blowpipes closed years ago and so did the general store where John bought the rope for the lighthouse tree. Just to the north of St Martin's Church is Lowside, the oldest part of the village. Here there are narrow winding streets dating from the days when Bowness was a fishing village and next door to the New Hall Inn the sharp-eyed explorer will spot the old smithy visited by Dick and Mr Dixon.

My favourite viewpoint from which to see this part of Ransome's Lakeland is Biskey Howe. This can be easily reached by leaving the shops and following Helm Road for a quarter of a mile, past the Windermere Hydro to the top of the hill. Here a signposted and a level footpath suitable for wheelchair users leads to a rocky outcrop. From the rocks there is an excellent view across the lake to a panorama of distant mountains, and in the other direction to the Windermere Ferry and the foot of the lake. There are plenty of seats, and a little exploration will disclose the well-worn steps cut in the rock to enable Victorian ladies wearing long skirts to reach the highest point.

The prospect of Long Island and the distant shore opposite the Bowness promenade has changed very little since Ransome's day. It is best seen in the early morning before the lake wakes up. The bay, with its Victorian steamer pier, landing stages and rowing boats, is still Rio Bay. A short walk behind the large building which has replaced the Victorian boatyards to the south of the bay itself brings the head of the lake into view. In the channel between the shore and Long Island are two rocks, the strangely named Curlew Crag and Hartley Wife. Ransome renamed them Hen and Chicken – names which he borrowed from real rocks to be found in the bay south of the ferry.

At the end of the modern boating complex, a footpath leading off the road. heads away from the crowds to the National Trust property of Cockshot Point. This is the northern promontory of the Holly Howe Bay, overlooking Long Island, with the south basin of Windermere stretching far into the distance. Ramp Holme occupies a prominent position where we would expect to see Wild Cat Island, and for that reason alone may have contributed something to its creation. A little way along the shore of the bay towards the ferry is a single boatshed belonging to the Scott family. It was Sir Samuel Scott who owned *Esperance* in Ransome's time. They moored *Esperance* a little way off-shore and used her as a houseboat. Near the ferry are some boatsheds. Here George Walker looked after racing yachts and kept an eye on *Swallow,* and I understand his grand-daughter carries on the business today.

Another nautical link with the lake that Ransome knew is the 'steamer' *Tern* which still carries her share of visitors on Windermere, just as she has done since 1891 when she was licensed to carry over 600 Victorian tourists. She was refurbished to mark her centenary and looks much as she did when Clifford Webb drew her, although nowadays the vessel is limited to 250 passengers. The tall, thin smoke-stack is misleading, however, as the vessel was converted from steam power to diesel in 1958. From her deck on the voyage to Lakeside it is possible to have a good look at Silver Holme (or Cormorant Island). The island does not match Ransome's drawing due to its lavish covering of trees. Another way to see Cormorant Island is by using a public footpath that follows the western shore for a short way. North of Silver Holme is Lazy Bay, surrounded by trees and quite difficult to pick out. This, of course, is just as it should be if it is the original of Horseshoe Cove. Nearby is Grass Holme, looking like a floating Peak of Darien.

Those with their own boats wanting to get afloat on Windermere will find the public slipway near the ferry a convenient launching place. Unpowered craft can be launched from the western shore (owned by the National Trust) behind the islands, and from the Trust's Fell Foot Park, which is situated opposite Lakeside at the south of the lake. There is also a slipway at the very head of the lake by The Wateredge

Hotel. A forty-five minute cruise from Bowness Bay goes round all the islands off Rio and passes through the narrow channel west of Long Island which was chosen by John during the race with *Amazon*.

There is no sign of Cache Island in the northern basin of Windermere, but the head of the lake itself is very much as Ransome described it in *Winter Holiday* and *The Picts and the Martyrs*. Explorers must make up their own mind about the site of the North Pole. On the flat grass of Borrans Park, about fifteen yards from the shore, enthusiasts have set a tablet to mark the spot where the dowsing revealed whatever it was that the dowsing did reveal. Above and beyond the road is Ambleside Park where there was once a Victorian conservatory that looked just how I had imagined the North Pole. On the other side of the mouth of the River Rothay are two possible Dariens standing at the head of a deep bay leading to Brathay Hall. It is the only deep bay on Windermere or Coniston similar to the one Ransome mapped for Holly Howe Bay, and the little cliffs offer a striking view of the lake stretching away towards the islands. Is it Darien – who knows? A little way up the River Rothay is the bridge used by Dorothea on her way to buy the cookery book in Ambleside

Ransome's home at Low Ludderburn can be reached from Bowness by taking the A5074 to Winster village and then turning right along the narrow lane for a mile to the River Winster which Ransome loved to fish. The river should be crossed by the ford and the rising road followed for half a mile before a left turn is for Low Ludderburn. This is the road Ransome 'crawled' along with a broken ankle after his fall. There is space to park one car beside the road a hundred yards or so before the cottage is reached. Low Ludderburn itself is easily found as the name appears on the gate. Outwardly it has changed very

little since the time when it was the home of the Ransomes, except that the yew trees have grown and the garden has matured. In February the orchard is still carpeted with the snowdrops that so delighted them when they first saw the cottage. Helen Caldwell who lives at Ludderburn, showed me over the cottage with its low ceilings and head-threatening beams. So thick are the walls of the cottage that a small stone staircase was built within one of them. The upper story of the barn where *Swallows and Amazons* was written is a large airy room with a fine polished wooden floor added by the Ransomes, and a wonderful view down the valley and into Yorkshire. Colonel Kelsall's signal station on the barn at Barkbooth can be seen less than a mile away, and may be reached by following the winding lanes. While I was at Ludderburn, Mrs Caldwell showed me some of the collection of bismuth bottles that Ransome had bought to ease his internal problems. These had been dumped at the bottom of the garden

'Visitors think gates and walls are just made for them to goggle over,' said Peggy in *Pigeon Post*. We should restrict ourselves to the role of Squashy Hat and respect the privacy of the folk who live in houses where there is a Ransome interest.

Ransome's desk, his typewriter and the various keepsakes that he liked to have around him are on show in the Abbot Hall Museum of Lakeland Life and Industry in Kendal. The room, which is laid out to resemble a study, contains many items given after Ransome's death by Evgenia, including some best-loved books, pictures, fishing rods and a chess set.

Two of Ransome's favourite inns, the Hark to Melody in Haverthwaite and the Red Lion at Lowick Bridge may be visited on the way to the rest of Ransome country. The Ransome's final home, Hill Top at Haverthwaite, is a large square house which stands overlooking the Rusland valley. It appeared to be some sort of a kennels when I was there. Hill Top can be reached by crossing the River Leven at Newby Bridge, turning left and left again after half a mile.

A quarter of a mile beyond Hill Top the road joins the valley road leading north to Rusland. Three miles further up the valley is Rusland Church, lying between beautiful rolling hills. It is a wonderfully quiet and peaceful place. In a corner of the churchyard, beneath the pine tree Ransome chose for their final resting place, is a simple stone memorial to Arthur and Evgenia.

We can retrace Ransome's boyhood journey on the wagonette from Greenodd Station, by driving from Greenodd up the valley of the Crake to the Red Lion, the inn where the charcoal burners used to leave new clay pipes for Ransome ninety years ago. Lowick Hall is only half a mile from the Red Lion, but as it cannot be seen without entering private property, it is scarcely worth a detour. Instead, turn right and cross the River Crake before turning left and following the narrow road to Nibthwaite and Swainson's Farm. Be warned – there is space for only one car to park beside the telephone box at Nibthwaite. Beside the white cottage near the telephone is the tiny bridge beneath which Arthur tickled trout. Swainson's, or Laurel House as it is now called lies a short distance up the track which leads to Bethecar. It looks nothing like Ransome's illustration, but the rear of the house has a cross-passage like that mentioned in *Swallowdale*. Beside Laurel House the path forks and the right-hand branch leads upwards. After about 150 yards it is possible to see down to the lake and the boathouse where Arthur and his brother and sisters played. Allan Tarn is very noticeable: a circular reed-fringed pool with a scattering of water-lilies. A little further exploration along the path will reveal the fearsome-looking Knickerbockerbreaker down which young Arthur slid.

A little further along the road a public footpath crosses private land to the lakeshore and the boathouse. This is the place where Ransome used to perform a secret rite:

> Without letting the others know what I was doing, I had to dip my hand in the water, as a greeting to the beloved lake or as a proof to myself that I had indeed come home. In later years, even as an old man, I have laughed at myself, resolved not to do it, and every time I have done it again.

Do not leave Nibthwaite in a hurry: it is pure Ransome country.

A mile or so up the lake the road which runs along the eastern side of Coniston Water reaches the shore at Low Peel Near. Here there is room to park, and from the beach nearby we have launched our small dinghy on expeditions to Wild Cat Island. The island itself is tantalisingly out of sight behind two small bays that some have seen as possible Horseshoe Coves, and the little cliff known as High Peel Near. The land between the road and the shore belongs to the National Trust, and as there are several footpaths leading towards the shore, it is a matter of simple exploration to reach a place where it is possible to look across the water towards the island's hidden harbour and the landing place. On the shore opposite the landing place there is a small beach which makes an ideal place to land when ferrying passengers to and from the island. It was from this beach that Collingwood's youngest daughter, Ursula, swam to the island with the proofs of Ransome's book, *Edgar Allan Poe,* fastened to her head, in order that Ransome, who was camping on the island, might correct them. In winter it is just the place to become Dick or Dorothea for a moment,

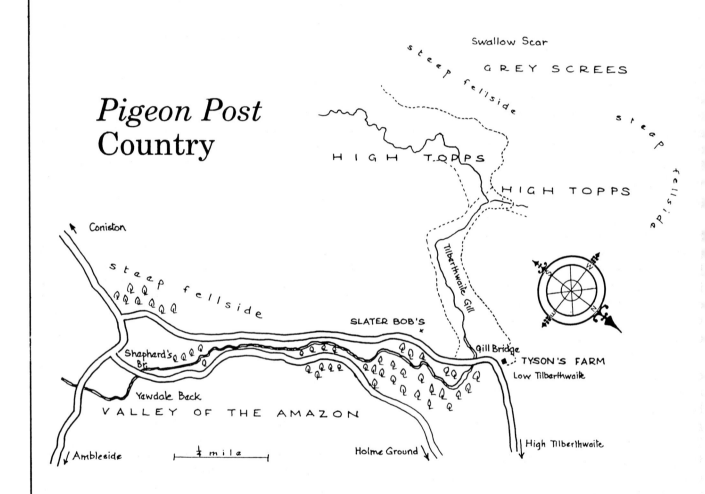

*Pigeon Post*
Country

Swallow Scar

GREY SCREES

steep fellside

steep fellside

HIGH TOPPS

HIGH TOPPS

Coniston

steep fellside

Tilberthwaite Gill

SLATER BOB'S

Gill Bridge

TYSON'S FARM

Low Tilberthwaite

Shephard's Br.

Yewdale Beck

VALLEY OF THE AMAZON

Ambleside

¼ mile

Holme Ground

High Tilberthwaite

standing at Dixon's landing place at the beginning of *Winter Holiday*.

Further north the road reaches the shore again and from here it is possible to look back at Peel (or Wild Cat Island). The steep woodlands on the other side of the road should not be ignored by explorers because at the southern end of Rigg Wood there are rows of tall larch trees, and just within sight of the road itself is a possible igloo. It is almost within sight of the island itself and well within the reach of Arthur's exploration from Nibthwaite. Whether the ruin was once a bark-peeler's hut, or that of a charcoal burner, I cannot say. The ground beneath the trees in the steep woodlands along the eastern side of Coniston is peppered with charcoal burners' pitsteads.

Mid-way along the lake is The Heald, a long stone bungalow of grey Coniston stone with a roof of green tiles from Coniston Old Man. The bungalow is half hidden among the trees and behind a high wall and is not easy to see. When Ransome lived there he owned half a mile of the lakeshore and 17 acres of woodland. 'Your son is once more a lake country land owner,' Ransome boasted to his mother.

A little further along the road are some foresters' cottages and beyond them, a footpath leaves the road and leads into the heart of Grizedale Forest. The path branches a couple of times, but by keeping to the right-hand track it is possible to enter the world of *The Picts and the Martyrs*. Ransome's description of the path is perfect: '. . . something like the bed of a dried-up mountain stream, sharp-edged stones and rocks with here and there a tiny pool'. Peggy was quite right about the wetness of the path after heavy rain, and it is easy to imagine old Cook stumbling up, carrying a half-finished pie dish. A beck does indeed cross the path, and just around another bend is The Dogs' Home itself, looking almost exactly like Ransome's drawing. Of all the Ransome places I found, this was perhaps the most satisfying to discover. When I eventually came upon it after a long search, it was occupied by an elderly squatter and the place was filthy. Once he had been removed, members of The Arthur Ransome Society nobly cleared it all up.

After passing Brantwood, the road reaches the Collingwood family home of Lanehead. Today it has a useful role as an Outdoor Education Centre for Cleveland Education Committee, but the house itself has a detached look and it is not easy to visualise Ransome bouncing along the lane to call up to Dora and Barbara at the window, 'Talking to you is like eating a strawberry ice'.

Bank Ground Farm is halfway down the fields which slope towards the lake. The side of the building presenting itself to the road does not look like Ransome's illustration. The building is L-shaped and the other wing may be seen at close quarters by taking the footpath which leads back across the fields from the road beside Tent Lodge, a quarter of a mile up the road. Aided by Ransome's headpiece for Chapter One of *Swallowdale*, identification is a simple matter, although in recent years there has been some modernisation of this wing, as Mrs Lucy Batty – the present-day Mrs Jackson – runs a friendly guest house and lets holiday flats.

Before Tent Lodge is reached, the road passes How Head Cottage where the whole Ransome family stayed for three weeks in 1905 at the time when Ransome was in love with Barbara and Dora Collingwood. Tent Lodge itself is worth a second look, as it could very easily have a place in Beckfoot's creation. Viewed from the lake it does have the correct number of windows!

The village of Coniston does not figure in the Swallows and Amazons stories, but The Ruskin Museum should be visited – if only for the wonderful sculpted head of Dora Collingwood by her sister Barbara. There are plans to extend the museum and a further possibility is that, when completed, it will house Ransome's *Coch-y-bonddhu* dinghy. Since he sailed *Cocky* on Coniston Water and she was used as a model for *Scarab*, it would be an appropriate location. A few years ago *Coch-y-bonddhu* was discovered in a very bad way in the grounds of a Strontian hotel in Scotland. Once again enthusiasts from all over the world responded generously to an appeal and ensured that it has been possible to make a complete restoration.

From Coniston village there are several ways to climb Coniston Old Man or Kanchenjunga. I prefer to take the road which starts by The Black Bull and soon becomes a rough path beside the great ravine of Church Beck. Miners Bridge, where Collingwood came upon Ransome writing poetry, is just above the main waterfall. The valley opens out at this point and a footpath on the other bank leads across the open fell to meet the quarry track. From this point it is a long, stony climb up through the desolation of the old mine buildings and spoil heaps to Low Water Tarn.

A longer way, avoiding the worst of the old quarries, and more nearly the route chosen by Nancy, is to ignore the bridge and follow the track past the distinctive white Coniston Coppermines Youth Hostel. Here, iron and copper pyrites or 'fool's gold' may still be found among the rough stones of the track and spoil heaps which disfigure, or add interest, to the region depending on your point of view. The path follows Levers Water Beck and passes in front of the youth hostel, shortly after which the half-way camp comes into view. From here, Coniston Old Man, Brimfell (where Roger saw wild goats) and Swirl How form

an impressive semi-circle of mountains just as Ransome described.

The track which leads to Levers Water should be left by a wooden footbridge, shortly after passing some mine entrances. From here a mainly level footpath returns to meet the quarry path after passing the Pudding Stone beside another wooden footbridge. The old pipeline running up the fell used to supply compressed air for Oscar Gnosspelius and John (Willie) Shaw's final attempt to mine for copper in the 1920s. The mine was high above Boulder Valley, beneath the shoulder of Brimfell.

After the hard stony climb through the quarries, the strikingly blue Low Water Tarn is just the place at which to relax, before making the steady forty-minute climb up the footpath to the summit cairn. Unfortunately, the final part, up which John and Nancy raced, has become so eroded that it is now a stony trench. The Swallows and Amazons were very fortunate to have such a clear day, for only once, in a score or so climbs, have I seen the Isle of Man from the top. Modern readers may wonder why Titty named the mountain Kanchenjunga. At the time of the Swallows and Amazons ascent Kanchenjunga in the Himalayas was in the public eye, as there had been attempts to climb the mountain in 1929 and 1930. Photographs of the mountain had appeared in the *Manchester Guardian* at the time Ransome was writing his Saturday articles. The mountain was first climbed in 1955 by George Band and Joe Brown and another pair, though in deference to locals who believed a saintly deity lived on top, they did not take the final step to the very crest of the summit.

Novice fellwalkers are advised to use the OS Outdoor Leisure map of the South Western Lake District, drawn to a scale of 1:25,000, and to take some additional clothing, as the temperature on the summit can be as much as 10 degrees Celsius below that in Coppermines Valley two thousand feet below. The shortest descent is to follow the Swallows and Amazons example and take the path all the way to Miners Bridge and the village.

The *Pigeon Post* country may be reached by leaving Coniston and following the A593 northwards for a mile and a half to High Yewdale. Low Yewdale (or Dixon's Farm) can be seen a short distance from the road on the right-hand side. At High Yewdale the main road passes over Yewdale Beck, but before this is reached a narrow turning leads to Tilberthwaite. Yewdale Beck forms the upper reaches of the River Amazon. The high ground to the west, marked on the maps vaguely as Above Beck Fells or Coniston Moor, is High Topps itself. In order to link this stretch of country with the existing Coniston Old Man/Kanchenjunga area already familiar to readers of *Swallowdale*, Ransome had to create his country in a mirror image of the real geography.

The narrow road taken by the dromedaries and described clearly by Ransome, is to be found on the north side of the beck. A car may be parked a few yards up this road at Shepherd's Bridge and the route of the dromedaries followed on foot. The road goes up the beck for about a mile and provides excellent views across the valley to Slater Bob's Mine, High Topps and Grey Screes. Unfortunately it does not cross the beck to Tyson's Farm, but leads away instead towards Holme Ground.

In order to reach the places on the other side of the beck, the Tilberthwaite road must be followed as far as Low Tilberthwaite, where there is space for several cars to park near the bridge. The road crosses Tilberthwaite Gill Bridge and passes what surely must be the original Tyson's Farm: a whitewashed cottage and a barn over the cow-house, sheltering beneath the fells which rise steeply behind it. Ransome avoided mentioning the spinning gallery which would have been too much of a give-away.

Slater Bob's Mine can be reached by returning along the road for about 200 metres until a path climbs up the fell towards the spoil heaps and old buildings mentioned in *Pigeon Post*. A little exploration will reveal Slater Bob's Mine entrance, or more properly, Horse Crag Level. Nowadays there is a gate in the mouth of the tunnel, for the mine was reopened in 1990 and is worked at weekends by George Tarr, who produces floor tiles. The tunnel is clear for 160 metres, and on the way it passes through a large cavern or underground slate quarry. It was here the prospectors found Slater Bob at work.

In 1933, after the final attempt to mine for copper had failed, Oscar Gnosspelius set up John (Willie) Shaw to mine for slate in Horse Crag Level. Shaw was working at the mine when Ransome visited the area with Oscar Gnosspelius in search of information on mining and local colour for *Pigeon Post*.

Tilberthwaite Gill is a spectacular waterfall deep in a tree-lined ravine which was particularly favoured by Victorian tourists seeking the spectacular and awe-inspiring. High Topps can be reached by paths either side of the ravine. I prefer the one which starts from Low Tilberthwaite. This whole area is riddled with old mines and is possibly the most dangerous corner in the Lake District. The deep vertical shafts and unsafe tunnels should be given a wide berth, and explorers should leave small children and dogs behind. Having reached High Topps, you will probably find it rather wetter underfoot than the prospectors did during the draught, but it is a wild piece of country and fully lives up to expectations of *Pigeon Post*.

Traditional wooden launches, named appropri-

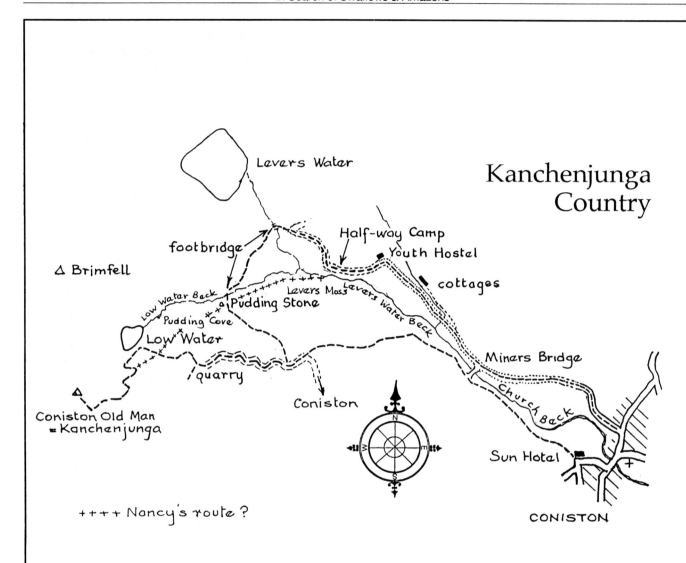

Levers Water

Kanchenjunga
Country

footbridge

Half-way Camp

Youth Hostel

△ Brimfell

cottages

Low Water Beck

Levers Moss

Levers Water Beck

Pudding Stone

Pudding Cove

Low Water

quarry

Miners Bridge

Coniston

Church Beck

△

Coniston Old Man

Kanchenjunga

N

W          E

S

Sun Hotel

CONISTON

+ + + + Nancy's route?

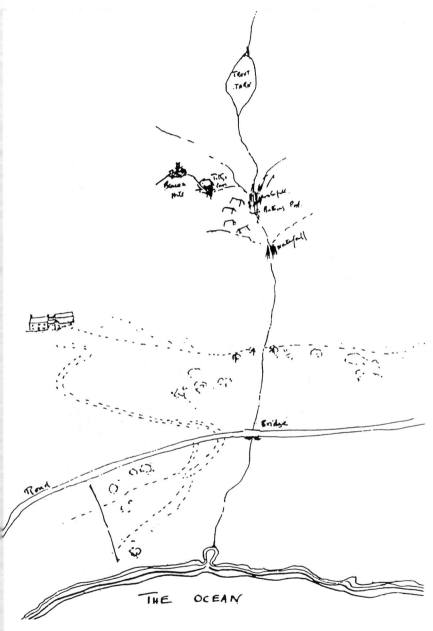

**Sketch map of Swallowdale by Arthur Ransome**

ately enough, *Ruskin* and *Ransome*, cruise to the head of the lake and down to Brantwood and Torver, giving excellent views of Tent Lodge, Lanehead, Holly Howe, the Holly Howe boathouses and The Heald.

Beckfoot has been variously identified as Lanehead, Tent Lodge or Seven Gates at Ambleside, and no doubt there are others. A mile or so beyond the village of Torver, the A5084 crosses Torver Beck at Sunny Bank and Oxen House shortly before reaching the shore of Coniston Water. It seems to me the origin of Beckfoot is to be found here. Oxen House is close to the right bank of a little river and 150 metres from its mouth. Like Beckfoot, it is also situated beside a road running near the lake shore and has a lawn running down to its boathouse. At one time there was a stable block across the yard. Further credence comes from its situation. Oxen House lies just across the water from Peel Island, and consequently part of the boyhood playground that Ransome evoked in *Swallows and Amazons*.

The remaining area that Ransome drew upon for his stories, lies to the west of Coniston Water between Blawith and Torver near Beacon Fell. He sketched out a rough map of Swallowdale, and apart from a little pulling about and simplification, it closely resembles the real geography. 'Beacon Hill' occupies a prominent position and Ransome probably omitted it from the story in order to preserve his secrets, as a link with Beacon Fell could readily be made by the curious reader armed with a map of Coniston.

A little over a mile beyond Oxen House there is space for a couple of cars to park beside a beck. There is no bridge, as the beck flows through a pipe beneath the road. Until the Civil Engineer's department tarred the road and levelled the bridges, there used to be a humpbacked bridge under which Titty and Roger could very well have crept. The beck leads to a small bay with one excellent headland – not the Horseshoe Cove of *Swallows and Amazons*, – for there is a difference between that and the Horseshoe Cove of *Swallowdale*, with its emphasis on the headlands or 'points'.

On the others side of the road is a large area of open moorland known as Blawith Fells. Swallowdale lies beyond the skyline and may be found by following the beck as closely as possible. In summer the bracken grows high, and the sheep tracks used by Titty and Roger are tempting, but do not always lead in the right direction. Explorers will not stray too far if they can still hear the sound of the beck and the noise of the waterfall. The lower waterfall fits Ransome's description and should satisfy the most demanding of pilgrims. The valley itself may be reached by climbing round the right-hand side of the large rock, down which water pours after heavy rain. Less than a hundred metres away at the head of the valley is another waterfall. The floor of the valley is flat, covered with bracken and inclined to be marshy. Apart from having a splendid Knickerbockerbreaker, the valley does not fit Ransome's drawing very well and some people are disappointed. It is worth remembering, however, that Ransome produced the illustration several years after the book was published.

Clifford Webb's drawing has captured the look of the place admirably. In my exploration I have walked for miles over Blawith Fells, as well as visiting half a dozen possible sites in the area suggested by other enthusiasts. Nothing I have seen matches Ransome's text so well, and no nearby waterfall rivals the splendour of the lower falls.

**Swallowdale, by Clifford Webb** (from **Swallowdale**)

The valley lies in a north-south direction and is called Long Scars on the maps. Perhaps Ransome rotated it through ninety degrees for the sake of simplicity. At the northern end there is a a Watch Tower Rock giving a fine view of Peel Island and the length of Coniston Water. The valley was formed by the same fault in the rock that occurs in the hidden harbour on Peel Island and it lies exactly in line with the Knickerbockerbreaker rocks. These rocks were of use to Ransome again in *Pigeon Post* where they fit the description of The Great Wall at the edge of High Topps, and the valley itself probably made another appearance as Golden Gulch.

Another valley favoured by some as the original Swallowdale lies ten miles away near Wastwater. Miterdale, however, has no lower falls, and the identification appears to be based solely on its similarity to Ransome's illustration, although even its supporters admit that it *is* rather large.

A little over half a mile from Swallowdale is Beacon Tarn (or Trout Tarn), a favourite picnic spot of the Altounyans, who sometimes swam there. This is one of the most beautiful of all the lowland tarns, having a backcloth of distant peaks – Coniston Old Man, Dow Crag and Brown Pike – to the north, and a low skyline looking towards Morecambe Bay to the south. There are several footpaths leading from the road to the tarn. Alternatively, it is possible to reach the tarn directly from Swallowdale by walking west, ignoring sheep tracks and avoiding the boggy ground. The summit of Beacon Fell is a short climb from the tarn and gives an even better view of the mountains and the lower fells to the north-west that Ransome called High Moor.

Seen from Beacon Fell, Peel Island occupies a prominent position on the lake and is a favourite rendezvous for canoeists. Rowing and motor boats may be hired at Coniston where there is a launching site. Unpowered craft may be launched from Brown How and Monk Coniston car parks. Motor boat (What would Captain John have said?) users should be particularly careful if they try to enter the harbour. A couple of years ago we had to salvage a couple of Japanese enthusiasts who had driven their hired motor boat on the rocks extending beyond the western arm of the harbour and stuck fast!

Peel Island is everything it should be – a little rocky paradise with miniature hills and valleys, sheltering beneath a canopy of trees. In the years to come a lighthouse tree, planted by members of the Arthur Ransome Society, should grow to take its proper place at the north end of the island. A matter of real concern is the growing number of fires which are being lit. Some years ago an expanse of heather on the eastern side was burnt and The National Trust, which owns the island, has put up a notice forbidding fires. It would be dreadful if some idiot set the whole island ablaze. The Altounyans knew about the danger of fires and used to picnic on the south-east corner of the island, on the top of the rock, well away from overhanging trees.

Another worthwhile voyage of discovery is to drift down the River Crake to Allan Tarn (or Octopus Lagoon), as it is not possible to reach the tarn without crossing farmland. It is a beautiful and peaceful place, and in among the water-lilies and reeds it can have changed little since Arthur and his brother and sisters played there.

Changes in the country about which Ransome wrote will occur from time to time, and enthusiasts will continue to debate the merit of various real locations. Because he created a landscape that was typical of the actual Lake District he knew, uncovering most of Ransome's secrets can only be a matter of educated guessing. Only this week I received a long letter explaining why Beckfoot is to be found near Pull Wyke Bay at the north of Windermere. How Ransome would enjoy it all! A few things, however, never seem to change. He would not be patient with any of us who go in search of his locations behaving – a regrettably some Lakeland visitors still do – like litter-louts or Hullabaloos: 'The road below this house,' he wrote from The Heald in June 1942, when petrol for private motoring was strictly limited by wartime rationing, 'is a steady stream of motor cars every weekend, carrying people with picnic baskets, who hurl their waste paper into my coppice.' Some fifteen years earlier, he was railing in his column in the *Manchester Guardian* against the Board of Trade for handing over the peace and beauty of Lake Windermere to a few rich men in fast motor boats by declining to impose a speed limit: 'There is no getting away from him. One man in a boat moving at 24 miles an hour can, in thirty minutes inflict himself on every other human being from end to end of the lake . . . trying with a tremendous accompaniment of noise and thrum to run away from his conscience.'

**Arthur Ransome, from a pencil sketch by Roger Wardale**

Bowness Bay

**Bowness Bay.** *Over there, beyond the pier they saw the long grey sheds, and slipways, and yachts hauled up in cradles, for scrubbing and painting and varnishing.* **Coots in the North.** (These Victorian boatsheds were pulled down more than 20 years ago.)

*Mavis* moored at Windermere Steamboat Museum

**Bowness Bay from Biskey Howe viewpoint**

**The Ransome Room at Abbot Hall.** (Photo: courtesy Abbot Hall Art Gallery and Museum)

**Arthur Ransome's desk at Abbot Hall**. (Photo: courtesy Abbot Hall)

Nibthwaite

**Nibthwaite 1995. Children beside the old stone jetty where Arthur Ransome and his brother and sisters used to play.**

ow Peel Near, Coniston Water

**Coch-y-bonddhu.** *Coch-y-bonddhu afloat once more, following the successful restoration in 1995.* (Photo: Robin Anderson)

**Windermere.** *For a long time they saw no more of the lake. Then, suddenly, they caught sight of it again, shining far away beneath them, reflecting the steep green woods on the further side.* **Coots in the North**

# Bibliography

*Works consulted or quoted in this book:*

Taqui Altounyan, *In Aleppo Once*. John Murray, 1969.

Taqui Altounyan, *Chimes from a Wooden Bell*. I.B. Taurus, 1990

Hugh Brogan, *The Life of Arthur Ransome*. Jonathan Cape, 1984.

Dora Collingwood, unpublished journal. Abbot Hall Art Gallery and Museum.

W.G. Collingwood, *The Lake Counties*. Dent 1902. (Revised edition 1932.) (New edition, revised by William Rollinson 1988.)

John Dawson, 'Swallows and Amazons', *Lancashire Life*. September 1988.

Christina Hardyment, *Arthur Ransome and Captain Flint's Trunk*. Jonathan Cape. 1984.

Eric Holland, *Coniston Copper Mines: A Field Guide*. Cicerone Press, 1981.

Eric Holland, *Coniston Copper*. Cicerone Press, 1986.

Peter Hunt, *Approaching Arthur Ransome*. Jonathan Cape, 1992.

Claire Kendall-Price, *In the Footsteps of the Swallows and Amazons*. Wild Cat Publishing, 1993.

Robert Bruce Lockhart, *Memoirs of a British Agent*. Putnam 1932.

Pauline Marshall, *Where it all Began* 1991.

George H. Pattinson, *The Great Age of Steam on Windermere*. Windermere Nautical Trust, 1981.

Arthur Ransome, *Pond and Stream*. A. Treherne, 1906.

Arthur Ransome, *Bohemia in London*. Chapman & Hall 1907.

Arthur Ransome, *Oscar Wilde*, a critical study. Martin Secker, 1912.

Arthur Ransome, *Old Peter's Russian Tales*. T.C. & E.C. Jack 1916.

Arthur Ransome, *Racundra's First Cruise*. Allan & Unwin 1923. (Reissued with an Introduction by C. Northcote Parkinson, Century Paperback, 1984.)

Arthur Ransome, *Rod and Line*. Jonathan Cape, 1929 (Reissued Oxford University Press paperback, 1980)

Arthur Ransome, *Swallows and Amazons*. Jonathan Cape, 1930. (Reissued with illustrations by Clifford Webb, 1931.) Reissued with illustrations by the author, 1938.)

Arthur Ransome, *Swallowdale*. With illustrations by Clifford Webb. Jonathan Cape, 1931. (reissued with illustrations by the author, 1936.)

Arthur Ransome, *Peter Duck*. Jonathan Cape, 1932.

Arthur Ransome, *Winter Holiday*. Jonathan Cape, 1933.

Arthur Ransome, *Coot Club*. Jonathan Cape, 1934.

Arthur Ransome, *Pigeon Post*. Jonathan Cape, 1936.

Arthur Ransome, *We Didn't Mean to Go to Sea*. Jonathan Cape, 1937,

Arthur Ransome, *Secret Water*. Jonathan Cape, 1939.

Arthur Ransome, *The Big Six*. Jonathan Cape, 1940.

Arthur Ransome, *The Picts and the Martyrs*. Jonathan Cape, 1943.

Arthur Ransome, *Great Northern?* Jonathan Cape, 1947.

Arthur Ransome, *Mainly about Fishing*. A. & C. Black, 1959.

Arthur Ransome, *The Autobiography of Arthur Ransome*. Edited and with Prologue and Epilogue by Rupert Hart-Davis. Jonathan Cape, 1976

Arthur Ransome, *Coots in The North*. Edited and with Introduction by Hugh Brogan. Jonathan Cape, 1988.

Arthur Ransome, *Arthur Ransome on Fishing*. Introduced by Jeremy Swift. Jonathan Cape, 1994.

Arthur Ransome, Letter to the Editor, Junior Bookshelf, 1936

Arthur Ransome, unpublished draft for his *Autobiography*, diaries, letters and manuscripts. The Brotherton Library, The University of Leeds.

Arthur Ransome, unpublished draft for *Swallows and Amazons*, his *Autobiography* and sketch-books. Abbot Hall Art Gallery and Museum, Kendal.

Hugh Shelley, *Arthur Ransome*. A Bodley Head Monograph. Bodley Head, 1960.

Alfred Wainwright, *A Pictorial Guide to the Lakeland Fells. Book Four The Southern Fells*. Westmorland Gazette, 1960.

Roger Wardale, *Arthur Ransome's Lakeland*. Dalesman Books, 1986.

Roger Wardale, *Arthur Ransome's East Anglia*. Poppyland Publishing, 1988.

Roger Wardale, *Nancy Blackett Under Sail with Arthur Ransome*. Jonathan Cape, 1991.

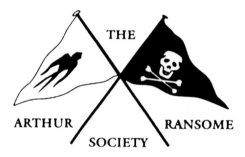

The Arthur Ransome Society aims to celebrate Ransome's life and to promote his works. A variety of meetings and activities are arranged by the six regional groups. There are three annual publications and regional newsletters. For more information, contact the Society: c/o Abbot Hall Gallery, Kendal, Cumbria LA9 5AL

# Index

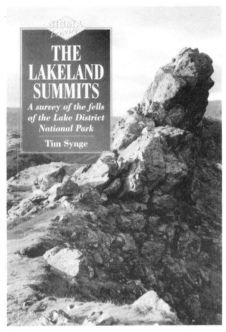

## WALKING LAKELAND TRACKWAYS: the Eastern Lakes
*Mike Cresswell*
*£7.95*

## THE LAKELAND SUMMITS: a survey of the fells of the Lake District National Park
*Tim Synge*
*£7.95*

## FULL DAYS ON THE LAKELAND FELLS: 25 challenging walks in the Lake District
*Adrian Dixon*
*£7.95*

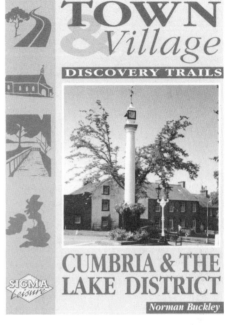

## LAKELAND ROCKY RAMBLES: Geology beneath your feet
*Bryan Lynas; Foreword by Chris Bonington*
*£9.95*

## PUB WALKS IN THE LAKE DISTRICT
*Neil Coates*
*£6.95*

## TOWN & VILLAGE DISCOVERY TRAILS: Cumbria & The Lake District
*Norman Buckley*
*£6.95*

## STROLLING WITH STEAM: Walks along the Keswick Railway
*Jan Darrall*
*£4.95*

## 100 LAKE DISTRICT HILL WALKS
*Gordon Brown*
*£7.95*

## LAKELAND WALKING: on the level
*Norman Buckley*
*£6.95*

## MOSTLY DOWNHILL: Leisurely Walks in the Lake District
*Alan Pears*
*£6.95*

All of our books are available from your local bookshop. In case of difficulty, or to obtain our complete catalogue, please contact:
SIGMA LEISURE, 1 SOUTH OAK LANE, WILMSLOW, CHESHIRE SK9 6AR
Phone: 01625 – 531035; Fax: 01625 – 536800
E-mail: sigma.press@zetnet.co.uk
Visit us on the World Wide Web –
http//www.zetnet.co.uk/coms/sigma.press/
ACCESS and VISA orders welcome – call our friendly sales staff or use our 24 hour Answerphone service! Most orders are despatched on the day we receive your order – you could be enjoying our books in just a couple of days. Please add £2 p&p to all orders.